Young at Heart

One day, as my mother approached her seventy-seventh birthday, she surprised me by saying, "Maxine, I hate to think that *pretty soon* I'll be old."

In my mind, seventy-seven was old!

But she wouldn't give in to age.

Look at your life. Do you consider yourself old? Have you passed fifty? or sixty? or seventy? It all depends on your outlook and the beckoning of still unconquered realms before you. Why not make a list of the things in life you'd like to do before you "get too old"? Would you like to learn to swim? Get a college degree? See Australia?

Don't let yourself withdraw from life. Just remember back a few decades when Frank Sinatra used to sing, "Young at Heart." You're not yet 105.

Neither am I, and "old" is older than me.

"Old" Is Older Than Me

Maxine Dowd JENSEN

Here's Life Publishers

First Printing, April 1991

Published by
HERE'S LIFE PUBLISHERS, INC.
P. O. Box 1576
San Bernardino, CA 92402

Library of Congress Cataloging-in-Publication Data
Jensen, Maxine Dowd, 1919- .
    Old is older than me : and other devotionals for the best years of your life / Maxine
Dowd Jensen.
        p.   cm.
    ISBN 0-89840-316-2
    1. Retirees—Prayer-books and devotions—English. 2. Aged—Prayer-books and devo-
tions—English. 3. Jensen, Maxine Dowd, 1919- . I. Title.
BV4580.J45   1990
    242'.65—dc 20   90-21257
                                     CIP

Cover photography by Deborah De Wit
Cover design by Cornerstone Graphics

Unless indicated otherwise, Scripture quotations are from the *King James Version*.
Scripture quotations designated NIV are from *The Holy Bible: New International Version*,
© 1973, 1978, 1984 by the International Bible Society. Published by Zondervan Bible
Publishers, Grand Rapids, Michigan. Scripture quotations designated TLB are from *The
Living Bible*, © 1971 by Tyndale House Publishers, Wheaton, Illinois.

For More Information, Write:
L.I.F.E. – P.O. Box A399, Sydney South 2000, Australia
Campus Crusade for Christ of Canada – Box 300, Vancouver, B.C., V6C 2X3, Canada
Campus Crusade for Christ – Pearl Assurance House, 4 Temple Row, Birmingham, B2 5HG, England
Lay Institute for Evangelism – P.O. Box 8786, Auckland 3, New Zealand
Campus Crusade for Christ – P.O. Box 240, Raffles City Post Office, Singapore 9117
Great Commission Movement of Nigeria – P.O. Box 500, Jos, Plateau State, Nigeria, West Africa
Campus Crusade for Christ International – Arrowhead Springs, San Bernardino, CA 92414, U.S.A.

TO MY MOTHER

*who showed me that the joy of living
can be interwoven with aging*

CONTENTS

SECTION III: Do Unto Others

SECTION IV: Home Is Where the Heart Is

SECTION V: Where Jesus Is 'Tis Heaven

SECTION I
ONLY AS OLD
AS YOU FEEL

1

"OLD" IS

OLDER THAN ME

READ: Genesis 17:15-19

Surely goodness and mercy shall follow me all the days of my life (Psalm 23:6a).

When I was thirty and my mother sixty-eight, we lived in a quaint house with high ceilings, a window above the bathtub and a tub that sat on little curved feet. My mother's fetish revolved around sparkling windows and crisp, full curtains. No matter how many times I told her, "Wait for me," after washing the window she would straddle the sides of that tub with the curtain rod and clean curtains in her hands.

One day, as she approached her seventy-seventh birthday, she surprised me by saying, "Maxine, I hate to think that *pretty soon* I'll be old."

In my mind, seventy-seven was old. Despite the fact that at least three times a week she walked more than two miles to a shopping center and "nosed around," as she called it, in the three large dime stores, despite the fact that she remained Works Chairman for our church's women's society, despite the fact that she opened her home and her heart for seminary students she felt didn't get the right kind of food in the school's cafeteria, I considered her old.

But she wouldn't give in to age.

Most of us age at different points. Nolan Ryan, in his forties, is old for a major league baseball player, yet his pitches are still clocked at more than ninety miles per hour. He continues to pitch no-hit games.

Mattie is twice as old as Nolan Ryan. Her tiny five-foot, two-inch body is crippled by polio and her hands are knobby with arthritis. And one more thing—Mattie plays the tuba. She currently performs not only in church but also as a member of a polka band. And if you need an accompanist, Mattie can sit down at the piano or organ and play nearly anything you place on the music rack.

Look at your life. Do you consider yourself old? Have you passed fifty? or sixty? or seventy? Much depends on your outlook and the beckoning of still unconquered realms before you. Why not make a list of the things in life you'd like to do before you "get too old"? Would you like to learn to swim? Get a college degree? See Australia?

Don't let yourself withdraw from life. Just remember back a few decades when Frank Sinatra used to sing, "Young at Heart." You're not yet 105.

Neither am I, and "old" is older than me.

PRAYER: Dear Lord, You know I'd like to keep active and alert to the very end of my life. Help me to plan enjoyable alternatives and strive for my dreams so that life will never lose its flavor for me.

2

THE HILLTOP

OF LIFE

READ: John 15:1-11

These things have I spoken unto you, that my joy might remain in you, and that your joy might be full (John 15:11).

One Sunday morning several years ago, I heard our pastor announce, "Tomorrow at 5:30 P.M., the Over-the-Hill group will meet for the first time."

My lower jaw tightened, astonishment and fire must have leaped from my eyes, and I clenched my fist.

Later I asked my cousin, "What did he mean 'over the hill'? We're the hilltoppers. Most of our children are raised and on their own. We are safe and comfortable in our chosen vocations. We've accumulated most of the essentials and gadgets we didn't have in our beginnings. Most of us enjoy good health. We now face our bonus years. We're on the hilltop of life!"

The group became "The Hilltoppers."

When we reach fifty-five and over, many of us have traveled fruitbearing avenues of service for

God. Some have enjoyed a constant abiding in Christ, and others no longer have any desire to yield to some of the temptations of our youth. If this is the case, why should we consider ourselves over-the-hill? This phrase connotes a cessation of joy in life.

If you know Christ as Savior, you are entitled to joy. Happiness fulfills a promise of God. It is a right of every believer, a right that should never cease.

If you are not enjoying your right of happiness, why aren't you? Perhaps some of the clues may be found in the Scripture reading for today. Perhaps you are a little short in the area of:

bearing fruit (verse 5);

abiding in Christ (verse 7);

keeping His commandments (verse 10).

Truly, the happiest years of your life may be just ahead.

PRAYER: Lord, if happiness is missing from my life today, help me to follow up on the clues in John 15 and trust You to restore my joy.

3

TO CHANGE
OR TO DECLINE?

READ: Isaiah 58:6-11

Thine health shall spring forth speedily
(Isaiah 58:8).

A ging brings change; it needn't bring decline.

Mental health is more important than physical health and man is limited only by his vision. None of the physical companions of aging need destroy our creativity nor our desire to *live* rather than simply exist.

Louis A. Crittenton, or "Dad Crit" as he was affectionately called, showed wisdom when he decided to enter the Maywood (Illinois) Baptist Home. This wisdom also evidenced itself when he asked for a room in the separate house on the grounds rather than in the more communal quarters. "I don't want to hear the shuffle of feet," he said.

Dad Crit never shuffled his.

Active in the Pacific Garden Mission in his youth and mid-years, he continued to be energetic until stricken with cancer in his mid-eighties.

I remember how, when I first came to his church as a young girl, this tall, white-haired man stooped to swallow my tiny hand in his two great sun-tanned ones as he boomed, "How are you, Girl?" Perhaps I'd never uttered a real prayer until I prayed for him.

He'd lost his wife to cancer, his home in trying to gain health for her, and his job of forty years. Then he lay ill in Cook County Hospital, a Chicago hospital for indigent people. These things happened shortly after we met but not before I'd grown to love him. I visited him in that hospital. His usually tanned skin was as white as the sheets and the walls that surrounded him. I prayed.

I heard his testimony to God's goodness at a weekly prayer service scarcely a month after his release from the hospital. I watched him rise again.

Perhaps his greatest ministry to young people came through his letters. Letters of encouragement for my writing and singing reached me with great regularity—sometimes the day after he'd just seen me.

He began speaking for the National Safety Council all over the midwest, but the letters continued coming. He spent a long period in California during WWII, traveling up and down the West Coast, lecturing about unity of purpose between management and labor and how to obtain this—and still his letters came.

Homesick himself, he went to the USOs where he not only played the piano but had personal talks about God with the service men and women. When they shipped out, his letters followed them.

To change or to decline? You have a choice. Find your special place or the special deed you can do for others. It will improve both your mental and physical health and leave the fragrance of you behind for others to remember after you've gone.

PRAYER: Oh Lord, as I grow older, lead me to a place or thing of service and give me joy in doing it.

4

COURAGE

TO AGE

READ: Ecclesiastes 5:1-3

The fool folds his hands and ruins himself
(Ecclesiastes 4:5, NIV).

Physical ailments come to all of us — if we live long enough. However, none of these can destroy our desire to live, unless we let them.

These thoughts are explored in *The Courage to Grow Old*, a collection of writings by forty-one prominent men and women, edited by Phillip L. Berman. Each person included believes he or she has a future. They all understand themselves and their world and they transmit the future they believe in to every reader. If you decide to look this book over, you, too, may find a belief in a rewarding future.

True, these days in the United States age is not respected much. Older individuals generally are not sought out for advice, and elderly citizens are often victimized. These conditions are due in part to the public's preoccupation with youth.

Yet growing older can be a time for expansion and liberation, a time of freedom never before experienced and hampered little by physical problems. Why, then, do some people fold their hands and indulge in self-pity?

To every suggestion made by friends to lift the clouds of her widow blues one woman replied with the words, "Oh, I couldn't do that." For at least seven years following her husband's death, she never invited a single friend in for coffee. "I can't entertain without Jerry," she would say.

She was in her early fifties and in good health. Her house was paid for by mortgage insurance, and she received an annuitant pension. She could have done anything or gone anywhere she chose. Instead, she decided to be contentedly discontent and let her friends wonder what they could do to help her. This woman's health began to fail as she indulged in her self-pity.

More and more the biblical truth of good health being a partial response to attitude and willingness to work for accomplishment is being accepted and utilized in the medical world. Doctors dealing with mental patients are awakening to these truths as well. Even meditation, such as Christians partake of when they read their Bibles and pray, is being approved by doctors and psychiatrists.

Old age may slow you down, but please don't let it stop you.

PRAYER: Lord, keep me from self-pity. I remember an adage my mother often used: "God helps those who help themselves." Help me to get up and get busy for You.

5

HOW OLD
IS OLD?

READ: Hebrews 11

Those whose faith has made them good in God's sight must live by faith, trusting him in everything (Hebrews 10:38a, TLB).

Many would have us believe that aging means an inevitable downhill road until we are crippled, incapacitated or mentally incompetent. This "ain't necessarily so," as the song says.

Prevention magazine has a walking program that many octogenarians—and older—are following. These senior adults are obtaining healthy weight statistics, more energy and an increase in stamina. Healthy bodies do not exclusively belong to the young.

Psychologists say that mental ability may slow as we grow older, but our logic and experience help us out and enable us to maintain high levels of intelligence equivalent to that of those who are many years younger.

The Senior's Week on the television show *Jeopardy* indicates that older adults can accumulate, store and remember many facts.

A ninety-three-year-old engineer I know is still working on inventions. He recently had an article published in a highly technical anthology. His only concession to age is a short nap every afternoon.

Mrs. Cook never revealed her age. At a church gathering, one member said, "I know how old you are. You're six months older than my mother—but I'll never tell."

"So I am," Mrs. Cook replied, "but don't you dare tell or the folks at the home won't let me go down to Chicago's loop on public transportation."

Though Myra and Burt are not physically perfect, probably no church has ever had as active a couple as members. On communion Sunday, rain or shine, they carry the bread and wine to a shut-in. The radio is tuned in to the service at church and the small group joins the congregation in breaking bread together. Myra and Burt find great joy in their service to the Lord.

Don't believe everyone who tells you to slow down or that you can't do this or that. Give it a try and trust the one who made that body and mind of yours.

PRAYER: Oh God, You made me; You've kept me so far. I trust You for my future years, be they ten more or forty more.

6

DARE

TO DREAM

READ: Philippians 4:10-13

*Joseph dreamed a dream and he told it to
his brethren: and they hated him the more*
(Genesis 37:5).

When we were young, like Joseph, most of us
dreamed dreams. It is one of the fortés of a
teenager. But in the metamorphosis to adult, we do
not all become the beautiful butterflies we imagined
we would. Instead, through circumstances beyond
our control or because we begin to believe our dream
was childish, we let the dream go. Sometimes we
forget it completely.

Some would say it is not possible to reactivate
your dreams when you start to age. It isn't? Then
why would anyone believe that the years after fifty-
five are bonus years? Edith Huey took a Sears
Roebuck camera to a photography course because
she wanted to learn how she could share the wild
flowers of Arkansas with others. When she revealed
her desire to the teacher, he gave her a conde-
scending smile and said, "Well, that's nice."

Edith succeeded—not with just one book but with others that followed. She says, "I couldn't have done this thirty-five years ago. I am more willing now to be myself, to do what I want."

The writer W. Somerset Maugham once said, "Imagination grows by exercise and, contrary to common belief, is more powerful in the mature than in the young."

Whether you are fifty-five and still employed or seventy and in your retirement years, ask yourself: What would I like to do with my remaining time? Perhaps now is when you should begin to refute the "old age" fallacy. Look back into your youth, unearth that dream, dust it off and start again.

PRAYER: Lord, we don't always know what things we are capable of doing until we try them. Help us to pray for guidance and to be venturesome enough to begin.

7

WHAT CAN
I DO?

READ: Exodus 3:10,11 and 4:10-12

Is anything too hard for the Lord?
(Genesis 18:14a).

Bonus years?" you may ask. "I feel more like I have a millstone around my neck."

Perhaps you've heard the words, "You're a good employee, but . . . " and you feel the rest of the sentence is "you're too old for the job."

You may *have* to work. Divorce, separation, illness, disability or death are situations that push some older workers back into the marketplace.

"What marketplace?" you may ask. "There's nothing out there for me."

That's not necessarily true. While physically we may not be quite as fast as we once were, we are more accurate; our reasoning power has improved; our various experiences have enriched and educated us; and we are often more reliable, honest and hard-working than many younger employees.

Lack of experience doesn't depend on age. It

can be a stumbling block in any period of life. At eighteen, Minette graduated from a junior college, but every employer wanted experience, not languages and history.

"I can't do anything," is an excuse, not a reason. You *can* do something. Look at your qualifications and desires. Make a list of them. How much schooling do you have? If you're a woman, did you ever work outside the home? What did you do? Did you like it? Now in your bonus years, or near to them, try to do things you like. Liking your job will enrich your life.

Some qualified people teach music or tutor in their homes. Some return to school and take courses that increase their job skills or teach them new ones. Some seek help from support groups.

Arkansas has a group called ABLE (Abilities Based on Long Experience). This agency promotes skills and confidence. A federally funded agency called Single Parent/Homemakers Career Development Agency works with people who find they must make a living for the first time.

Edith Cooper, sex equity and vocational counselor with the Single Parent/Homemakers programs, says, "More managers are becoming convinced that older women are good workers."

The Association of American Retired Persons has a senior Community Service Employment Program.

Check into this type of help in your area or state. You might be surprised at what you find.

These suggestions all may help, but we can

also elicit a special helper—God. I know. He's helped me in every job I've had, save one, and in every promotion. I must admit that the change of positions when I didn't seek His help is the only one from which I was fired.

PRAYER: Lord, I don't want to be useless, waiting around to die. I need to be used. You know all about me so lead me in the way I should go. Help me to remember that nothing is too hard for You.

8

WHY

WORRY?

READ: Matthew 6:28-34

Seek first his kingdom and his righteousness . . . do not worry about tomorrow, for tomorrow will worry about itself (Matthew 6:33a,34, NIV).

Mira Lindner, author of *Beauty Begins at Sixty*, says, "Forget about chronological age. What does it mean? You can be old at thirty and you can be very young at eighty."

I noticed this in my teens when we had two women in our church who'd been born in 1900.

I don't believe the one was ever young. She wore only shirtwaist dresses and kept her hair in a knot at the nape of her neck. No extra color touched the lips that rarely smiled, and she was a tattletale.

The other woman, Primrose, married for the first time at forty-eight. All of us young girls wanted to give her a beautiful wedding reception. Today, soon to be ninety, she has entered an "alive" life-care center in Arizona and is urging a friend of my mother to join her there. "We'll have fun," she told her.

Primrose still dresses up and rides a float in

the Christmas parade as Granny Noel, takes trips to far-away places like Australia and praises God for her health and strength. This lively women exudes joy.

I believe joy is the *right* of the Christian. It is more than just a privilege, and it can increase as we grow older. Search your Bible and you, too, will be assured of that truth.

Why, then, are many people not happy? Are you happy?

Do you fear the future? Your God knows the future.

Are you worried about financial needs? The Lord has promised to supply all of them. This doesn't mean He will give all we'd like to possess, but we are confident of having everything we need.

Does the prospect of possible ill health dog your steps? Receive a merry heart from the almighty and it will do you good like a medicine.

I called a recent widower a short time ago. He was coping with both the loss of his wife and his own health problems. Afterward, he wrote to tell me my optimistic encouragement had been like a dose of good medicine.

Share the joy you've found in the Lord with someone today.

PRAYER: Dear Lord, I long to bubble with delight over little things and to accept aging and yet look forward to the future. Help me ever to be confident of Your ability to make all things work for good in my life.

9

HALLELUJAH!

READ: Philippians 4:1-9

Let your gentleness be evident to all
(Philippians 4:5*a*, NIV).

A normally happy, optimistic woman sat at her forty-fifth birthday dinner with a glum expression on her face. When her husband asked her why she wasn't enjoying the special event, she said, "I've lived over half my life and I haven't left my mark on a thing."

Naturally, he tried to lift her spirits with words like, "Don't talk that way. You'll live a long, long time, honey."

"Not ninety years."

Many people suffer a midlife crisis. Men often seek younger women. They become restless and dissatisfied with their jobs, realizing they will never attain a top spot in their company. They feel chained to their mortgage, their family and their car payments. Women color their hair, visit a fat farm or have a face lift. Anything to halt the aging process.

Is change bad?

Changing wives or husbands goes against God's "until death do us part." But what about other changes?

Our bodies are the temples of the Holy Spirit. Therefore, inside and out, we should be in top shape. Some people will judge all Christians by the impression we make.

When a well-known Bible institute back in the thirties and forties had very stringent rules about makeup and dress, an older teenager was heard to remark, "They'd surely set a better example for Christ if they looked more alive with a little rouge and lipstick."

Do you look alive, vibrant, happy in the Lord?

If you plan to continue working for a number of years before deciding to retire, you may want to color your hair when the grey first appears — whether you're a man or a woman. To do this could increase your chances to go another step up the corporate ladder and retire with a better pension, and therefore, be able to continue your present plateau of living.

There's nothing wrong with change unless you throw moderation into a tornado's path or you waste money you can't afford to lose or you abandon God's basic laws.

The woman who was so glum on her forty-fifth birthday failed to count the teenagers who felt the hand of her Savior as she worked with them and the elderly friends of her mother whose faces brightened every time one of the letters or perky cards from her lay in their hands. She thought only of her lost dreams. She forgot she could still aim for her goals. God could still use her to move hearts—

and as long as she had health and a bit of money, she also could see the world.

Your dreams may not be as far away as you think.

The approach of retirement can give you the opportunities to change yourself, your priorities and your activities.

PRAYER: Lord, life isn't over for me just because I'm getting older and haven't done all the things I dreamed about. You can still help me utilize my abilities and bring joy to myself and to others. Hallelujah!

SECTION II
MAKE YOUR OWN
HAPPINESS

10

MAP OUT
A PLAN

READ: 1 Timothy 6:5-7

But godliness with contentment is great gain
(1 Timothy 6:6, NIV).

A retired supervisor once sent a cartoon to our office. It pictured an older man seated in the front yard beside a canopied table. A cool drink sat on the table. At the door to the house stood a man holding a clipboard and a woman who wore a bandanna and an apron.

"Retired couple?" asked the pollster.

"No," replied the woman, "retired man and his wife."

The office force laughed.

However, when my friend Karoline knew her husband planned to retire, she confided, "I don't know what I'm going to do with him underfoot every day. I won't be able to go to my clubs ... or ... or *anything*."

Lots of people, wives especially, have that fear.

It's wise to start thinking about that future several years before either of you reaches retirement age. Communicate. Spell out what you want your bonus years to hold.

Where do you want to live? Are your finances ready for retirement? Do you want to travel? Do you foresee any health problems? Would you like to learn how to paint or use a computer or speak a foreign language?

Set some goals now for your retirement years. Discuss expectations and begin to make your plans. And don't forget to speak with God. The Lord can supply wisdom to make your future echo Robert Browning's words:

> Grow old along with me!
> The best is yet to be,
> The last of life, for which the first
>   was made.
> Our times are in His hand.

PRAYER: Lord, help us plan our future believing the best is yet to come.

11

ENOUGH AND

TO SPARE

READ: Psalm 23

My cup runneth over (Psalm 23:5*b*).

There is "many a slip 'twixt the cup and the lip," but it never hurts to have the cup filled with plans and anticipated events even if they never become reality. Approaching retirement is the perfect time to fill the cup.

One main question is, How much money will I need in retirement? Because this is such a complicated and crucial issue, even age forty is not too early to look ahead and start making financial plans.

Don Underwood, a Merrill Lynch executive who's been in charge of its retirement planning section, says 75 percent of what you will earn your final year is probably what you will need in retirement. We are living longer, so our money must last for a greater period of time. Therefore, check your expenses now and see what 25 percent you can live without.

For most, money for daily use will be less necessary. Transportation and luncheon costs often diminish or stop altogether when you leave your job.

Both men and women may find they need to add more casual clothes to their wardrobe, especially those who've held executive positions or who've worked in an environment that required "professional" clothing. This added expense needs to be taken into consideration.

You may want to purchase some specific things just before you retire. Perhaps you'll want to buy a new Bible to start marking up in new ways. Minette purchased a Bible because her old one bore reminiscences of her working life and a new one would meet future needs. In addition, because it was a new version, she felt it would reveal refreshing insights into old passages. Nita replenished her stock of bed linens and towels. These items had lured her in her working days and "buying enough now at a white sale will last me the rest of my life," she said.

David purchased resource books he'd previously borrowed from the company library. Jim bought a Laymen's Parallel Bible so he could compare four different translations.

I agree with Mr. Underwood regarding the 75 percent that may be needed, but after requesting counsel from the Lord and following my anticipated plans, I started out with much less.

Our company pension plan had been revised the year before my husband died. I fulfilled the requirements so I took an early retirement to be with my husband who was ill. I was penalized 6 percent for each year I was under fifty-five, but I felt it was just. I would probably recoup most of it due to the extra years I would receive the pension.

My husband died within my first month on pension. My boss asked me to return to work since he'd not yet chosen a permanent replacement. I declined—I had other plans. I wanted to write.

Several months after my husband's death I moved into a home in Arkansas that we had bought for our retirement—considerably sooner than we had planned.

I bought a ledger book and kept meticulous records. I paid nearly everything by check. I needed to know where, if anywhere, I was overspending because I wanted to squeeze in some travel.

In my second full year of retirement, God enabled me to experience three springs: (1) the redbud, dogwood and other beautiful blooms of Arkansas; (2) the gorgeous southern bougainvillea and other unfamiliar flowers of Florida; and, (3) in the British Isles, the vistas of hanging fuschias, rhododendron trees, the deep yellow of the wicked thorned gorse, the waving fronds of Scottish broom, dainty shamrock blooms and England's May flower, and the rugged shades of brown terrain in Scotland.

I believe that you can do almost anything you really want to in retirement. It truly can be a God-led time filled with new experiences and exciting vistas.

PRAYER: Almighty God, I praise You because I don't have to wait to enjoy what lies before me. Open my eyes to every opportunity. Help me take advantage of these and lead me into rejoicing because of them.

12

GOD'S
MATH

READ: 2 Chronicles 13:3-18

I have been young, and now am old; yet I have not seen the righteous forsaken, nor his seed begging bread (Psalm 37:25).

It's easier to be poor when young than when you hit seventy," read a headline in the December 11, 1989, *Arkansas Gazette*. It was spoken by Verne C. Bates, Senior Vice President at Valley National Bank of Des Moines, Iowa. Do you believe it?

When young we think we are invulnerable: to ailments, to accidents and, in the thinking of many today, to addictions. At seventy we know otherwise.

The key to being richer at seventy than you might be is to plan *now*. According to a stockbroker named Brian Lasko, you only have four choices:

- Save more
- Increase your return on savings
- Delay retirement
- Accept a lower standard of living after retirement.

Most of us would prefer not to do the latter. Therefore, how can we avoid it?

IRAs still offer tax deferment if you have earned income. Lower income and higher risk is appropriate for younger individuals but in the mid-years this should be toned down to a 50/50 split, and in later years, a 70/30 range. It's also a good idea to remember the old adage, "Don't put all your eggs in one basket."

When we think of the above, we have to utilize mathematics. Did you ever notice that God's math doesn't work like ours? An example is in our reading portion for today. Four thousand men faced eight thousand men, and the former slew five thousand of the latter.

Perhaps some of us have noticed the difference because God's math has come to our attention when we've faced monetary insurmountables like feeding and paying bills for three adults on $9 a week.

One eighty-year-old I know is using God's arithmetic. After her basic apartment bills are paid, she lives on a balance of $66 per month for every-thing else — food, doctor bills, gas and other essentials. Sometimes a friend moves away and stocks her larder with things like foods she's never tasted before, cleaning supplies or various staples that would increase a moving bill. Dinner invitations have come when she's down to her last 50 cents and her pantry is empty. Space would be extended if you knew all the ways God keeps her cruse of oil and bag of meal filled.

Are you afraid of the future? Do you wonder

if your money will last until the end of your life?

God expects us to do all things in moderation. The Lord counts on us to be wise in using our material assets but we are also admonished to "take therefore no thought for the morrow: for the morrow shall take thought for the things of itself" (Matthew 6:34a).

Follow His commandments, believe His promises, then shout "Hallelujah!"

PRAYER: Oh Lord, forgive me for my fears and for worrying about tomorrow. Increase my faith in Your love, Your providence and Your continued care for me and my future.

13

LIFE AFTER
RETIREMENT

READ: Genesis 6:9 – 7:6

Noah was six hundred years old when the flood-waters came on the earth (Genesis 7:6, NIV).

Just because you've retired doesn't mean your working days are over.

After Bill's retirement, he and his wife Marge remained in the home they'd purchased twenty years before. They were looking forward to the freedom of retirement years. But now that he had all the time for himself he had wanted, Bill was bored.

A call surprised him one day. His company had decided to reclaim their willing retirees as consultants with no interruption in pension and retirement benefits.

Some employers are beginning to value the strong work ethic and the experience of older workers. Some are redesigning jobs, hours and work sites (sometimes in the employee's own home), and they are setting up phased-in retirement programs where workloads are reduced and spread over an extended period of time.

A veteran Grumman Corporation (Bethpage, New York) employee says his twenty-hour workweek program is preparing him emotionally for full retirement.

Will you be bored in retirement? Would you prefer to work at least part-time? Look into the new options becoming available. Find out if your company offers any programs like the ones mentioned above. Pray about your future. Be assured you don't have to look for a job as a short-order cook in a franchised fast-food company, unless that's something you'd like to do. You can, with God's help, find a job suited to your talents and your time wishes.

Don't be afraid of retirement.

PRAYER: Dear Lord, help me to know how to spend my retirement time. Lead me to those opportunities that will bring joy to my life and glory to Your name.

14

YOUR HEART'S DESIRE

READ: Amos 3:3-7

Can two walk together, except they be agreed?
(Amos 3:3)

"Max," my husband said one day, "with the change in the pension age rules, we're both eligible for retirement. Let's do it."

My heart skipped a beat. I hadn't thought of retiring—yet. My boss seemed on the brink of a step up; I'd probably go along on that promotion. I had just become eligible for early retirement which meant I'd take a 6 percent cut in pay for each of the five years I was under fifty-five. My husband, six years older and with more than forty years of service, would get his full amount.

I began thinking, *He's had to work since he was fifteen, sometimes adding a second job and, like me, rarely able to pursue his own special interests. Both of us have abilities we've never been able to use and interests we've never been able to follow as completely as we've wanted.*

So we discussed it.

The more I thought about retirement and the more we talked about it and prayed about it, the more I wanted it. *At last,* I thought, *I'll be able to pursue my lifelong dream.*

One night I told him, "There's something I'm going to do. I'm going to write three days a week, four hours a day. I'm not going to answer the telephone or doorbell or even kiss you during that time."

"Okay," he replied. "You can do that while I'm night fishing." This city husband of mine had some plans, too.

As you look into your past, you will discover something you either never had a chance to do or never could sacrifice enough time to pursue it as you would have liked. Your future can include that special thing.

PRAYER: Dear Lord, most of us don't want to grow old nor do we want to think of retirement. Help us look forward to the future knowing that You have readied enjoyable experiences for us regardless of our age or abilities.

15

OUT OF
ERRORS
COME LAUGHS

READ: Ecclesiastes 3:1-12

Wherefore I perceive that there is nothing better than that a man should rejoice in his own works (Ecclesiastes 3:22a).

In Edwin Arlington Robinson's poem "Ballade by the Fire" he says:

Life is the game that must be played.
This truth at least, good friends,
    we know;
So live and laugh, nor be dismayed
As one by one the phantoms go.

Have you ever known a person who laughed at *everything*? Probably not. Some things are not laughable—but most are, if you look for the humor.

Molly wanted to surprise her husband after they moved into their vacation and future retirement home. He always hung the curtains, the pictures—everything but the wash. So one day she decided to create a family "rogue's gallery" herself on a hall wall.

She arranged and rearranged the pictures on the guest room bed until she knew exactly how they were to be placed. The pictures hung straight on the first and second holders she hammered into the wall. However, as she hit the third holder, the first picture swung, hit the second one, and as she grabbed for them, the corner of one gouged a hole in the wall.

She slipped to her knees and started to cry. She'd ruined the wall.

Then as she thought about it, she began to laugh. *Silly goof*, she told herself. *Who knows what happened the first time HE tried to hang a picture?*

Starting over again, she found a way to hide the hole. When her husband admired her work, she shyly slid one picture aside to reveal her mistake to him.

PRAYER: God, only You know how many mistakes we creatures make. Help us to laugh when we can and seek a solution for every error.

16

THE PEOPLE
MATTER

READ: 2 Timothy 4:5-11

A friend loveth at all times (Proverbs 17:17*a*).

Thinking of home brings thoughts of family — the brother you loved, the sister who thought of no one but herself, the uncle who knew how to make you laugh when you were blue. Through the years, various circumstances, such as distance, failure to write or call, or hurt feelings, may have separated you.

A young woman named her first baby after her sister who was eight years older than she was. She traveled a thousand miles to show the older woman her baby but returned saying, "She never asked to hold her and scarcely even looked at her. My sister can come visit me, but I'll never go to her home again."

Though it's difficult to take the first step, ten years later this younger sister decided to do it. The relationship is not all it could be because the older woman hasn't changed much, but there is communication where once there was none. And that's the place to start.

The older we grow, I think the more we realize that it's the people who count. Unfortunately, we may let possessions or jobs or distances or misunderstandings or just plain selfishness get between us and the friends and family we love. The bonus years are the perfect time to refocus on the people who have been special to us.

Alita was my best friend in high school and junior college. We walked home together, we traded confidences, we vied for grades, and we shared many of our social activities. One of the Shakespearian passages she patiently listened to me memorize was Polonius's speech to his son. It became my favorite because of the words:

> Those friends thou hast, and their
>   adoption tried,
> Grapple them to thy soul with hoops
>   of steel.

When Alita moved to Florida letters kept our friendship alive but we only saw each other three times.

When I was widowed and planned to visit a daughter in Florida, I asked Alita if it would be convenient for me to visit her. The answer was yes.

Our visit was delightful.

When I was leaving, my friend said, "I wondered what our visit would be like after all these years. I found it just as though we'd walked home from school only yesterday."

When you retire, look up former friends from

home and renew these relationships. Mend any broken fences with your relatives.

Paul found new hope with John Mark. Fallow ground may become fertile once more as you reactivate these connections.

PRAYER: Lord, I realize it's the people who count. Friends seem to disappear and some of them die as I age. There are family members I've lost contact with due to unhappy circumstances. Help me to recover and reactivate those relationships.

17

ENJOY

ASTONISHMENT

READ: Acts 12:1-17

When they opened the door and saw him, they were astonished (Acts 12:16b, NIV).

You'll notice in today's Scripture passage that only Rhoda was without surprise at Peter's appearance. Instead, her gladness prompted her to run to tell the others—a natural reaction to the joy she felt at hearing Peter's voice. She didn't even open the outer door! Her first thought was to share the news.

Convincing the others that God had answered their prayers took some doing.

Today this reaction of surprised unbelief is repeated many times in the lives of Christians. We pray; we think we believe the Lord will answer; then we are astonished when He does.

The Lord quickly answered the petitions of those praying for Peter. You and I have had some prayers answered even while we were still praying, but long-awaited answers tend to dull our anticipation. They are the ones that seem to create amazement when the answer arrives.

Though I'm not always able to keep my expectations strong, in one recent happening I was able to.

More than ten years ago I tried to sell my house. Interest rates were high and the couple who wanted to buy it could not sell their own. Then five years ago, another prospective buyer reneged on the contract. Did this indicate God did not mean for me to move? Perhaps.

Still, God knew public transportation was non-existent where I lived. He also knew sources of research material had dried up in our region and I couldn't wait four months to receive a book I ordered and then find it to be of no help.

Did God sympathize with my frustrations? I believed He did.

Since I often talk to God as though He were sitting across the table from me, at the last failure to sell my house I said, "Lord, I guess this isn't Your time for my move. Therefore, I'll not put my house up for sale again, and when the time is right, You let me know by sending someone who *asks* to buy it." I relaxed.

About a year later, I heard the words, "Max, are you still willing to sell your house?"

I replied, "Any time."

They put their house up for sale. I said I would hold mine for them. We all waited but no prospects came to their place, not even lookers. I heard the plans they expected to carry out when my house was theirs, and occasionally they said to me, "Now, if you want to put your house up for sale, you do it because we're not having any luck."

My answer was, "I promised I'd hold it." And I held it for almost four years.

Three months ago, they finally sold their house. Although I continued to expect God to arrange things, I'll admit I did not expect His timing to be so perfect, nor the price to be so right. God took care of everything. I'm happy in my new location and so are they.

When you pray, remember God does answer. Your needs are known to Him — right down to the exact penny. Expect things to turn out right. And yes, sometimes be willing to wait awhile.

Praise Him and rejoice when you receive your answer. No matter what it brings, it will be God's will for your life at that particular time.

PRAYER: Lord, I'm often impatient. I want answers and solutions *now*. When they don't arrive immediately, I'm tempted to lose hope, and then I'm surprised when the request is met. Forgive me and help my unbelief.

18

CHANGE
CAN BRING
HAPPINESS

READ: Matthew 4:18-22

I had fainted unless I had believed to see the goodness of the LORD in the land of the living (Psalm 27:13).

Every day at the lunchroom table, Hilda complained about her job, the office atmosphere and the bosses. One day Maude, a younger, newer employee, said, "If you dislike your work so much, why don't you consider looking for a new job?"

Are you happy with your present job? If you think you'd like to change and you fret about it, you may be creating an unnecessary problem for yourself. This can deplete your energy, change your personality and cause a negative reaction toward you from those around you. The lack of enjoyment in your job affects the quality of your whole life.

Now that you are approaching or are in your bonus years, have you thought about changing vocations? Maybe starting one you think you would like more than anything you've ever done before? Has

Jesus "called" you? Have you been aware of His voice? What benefits, now missing, would you like to enjoy in another position?

A number of companies today offer incentives for early retirement. A comparatively new law allows workers to receive deferred pensions, providing the length of employment is adequate.

Some day soon, sit down and, under a "positive" column heading, itemize the fruits of the Spirit that characterize you and your abilities. Add a "negative" heading and make a column of unhappy or aggravating circumstances in your life. Then decide if it's worth trying to make a change in either your job or yourself.

Some people, after becoming disgruntled at the promotions being passed out or bored with their working tasks or when needing a higher salary because of home responsibilities, pray and seek a change. This change need not mean leaving your company. You can explore opportunities within your firm if you know your own strong points and are aware of other departments and how they operate.

Peter, Andrew, James and John were fishermen. If you've ever fished, you know that part of the joy is trolling softly through clear waters under a tender sky or gently swaying with the breezes in a partially hidden cove. You don't want a lot of noise or many people around. Sometimes the serenity of your site or the close familiarity of the darkness that surrounds you on a pier makes up for a poor catch.

These may have been some of the joys the disciples knew before Christ called them.

How different it must have been to be surrounded suddenly by thousands of people, to have to cope with loud voices and shoving bodies, to try to protect the Master from the excited crowds.

If Christ calls you as He did these men, will you be willing to change?

Some of us resist change out of fear. Hilda didn't seek a new job. She just kept complaining. Maude, the girl who had asked her the question, left the company several years later for an entirely different type of work. When she left, Hilda said to her, "I'd like to quit, too, but I'm afraid. I admire you and your confidence in yourself."

What she didn't know was that Maude's confidence came from faith in God and a trust stemming from that faith.

As we get older, we sometimes grow less venturesome. However, this is often the very time when our experience, our financial base and our faith can say, "Try it. You'll like it." Change often signifies growth. Change may bring new joys, new friends, a new zest for living. It's worth the effort.

PRAYER: Oh, God, sometimes I am afraid of the future yet unhappy with the present. Help me to determine if a change might be enriching. Then lead me into the path You'd like me to follow.

19

THE
THREE Rs
OF CHANGE

READ: Genesis 12:1-5

So Abram departed, as the LORD had spoken unto him (Genesis 12:4a).

Major work and life changes are common. However, three words and the practice of them can help us survive those changes and even thrive as a result of them. Those three words are:

- Recover
- Refocus
- Regenerate

Recover

After a change that is stressful, challenging or unfamiliar, you may experience physical symptoms such as headaches, backaches or depression. To get back on track, you need to get a new perspective. Plan a weekend getaway or take time just for yourself. Go to a concert or a movie like *Driving Miss*

Daisy. Exercise. Share your feelings with friends. It will start you on the road back.

Refocus

Get the big picture. Your feelings may be mixed:

You like your new location but you miss your friends.

The winter is snowy and you miss the beach.

You enjoy the challenge of your new work but you haven't yet found an inexpensive place to eat a good lunch.

The talk at relief time is stimulating but you aren't sure about the attitudes and personalities of your new coworkers.

The neighbors look interesting, but no one says more than hello.

Maybe you feel sad or angry about letting go of familiar routines.

It's time to step back and look at the overall picture. Do the positive features of your new residence or job outweigh the negatives? Usually they do.

You'll learn to know the neighborhood and the neighbors. If you are friendly, most of the people around you will become so, too. Perhaps you need to get out of the rut of your old ways of doing things.

Refocus and settle in.

Regenerate

Change can be stressful to your body. Therefore, you need to get extra rest and avoid doing or eating things that upset your mind or your body. Connect with the new people. Renew and reinforce old friendships. Rely on the Lord.

Accept the change and determine you will be successful in it.

PRAYER: Oh God, does everyone resist change? Help me to be like Abram, willing to follow Your leading. Help me to find the sunny side and the positive points in every situation even though I may not believe, at first, that there are any.

20

I'VE GOTTA
BE ME

READ: 1 Samuel 17:31-40

Then he took his staff in his hand, chose five smooth stones from the stream, put them in the pouch of his shepherd's bag and, with his sling in his hand, approached the Philistine (1 Samuel 17:40, NIV).

George Bernard Shaw wrote:
People are always blaming their circumstances for what they are . . . The people who get on in this world are the people who get up and look for the circumstances they want, and if they can't find them, make them.[1]

An example of this is Cedell Davis, a guitar playing, blues musician. He is someone who created the circumstances he wanted. Handicapped by polio, he used a butter knife for the chording on a didleybow when he was a child. He says, "I don't really expect that polio made much difference. You see, you can always solve a problem if you just think about it so you can understand it."

Circumstances can appear as "Philistines" in

1. George Bernard Shaw, *Mrs. Warren's Profession*, Act II (1893).

our lives. We may feel like the Israelites and respond as they did: hide out in the face of the giant. But, oh, the excitement of being a David! Grab your faith and some stones and rely on God to do the fighting for you.

Losing your beloved spouse may be the "Goliath" you're facing. Some men lose their wife at a fairly young age. Women usually become widows after their children are grown and have moved away. Some of these men and women forsake happiness.

Given time, though, there can be happiness if you get up and look for what you want. Think about your situation from a new angle. Janice Clark, a reporter and a painter, says about her situation as a widow, "For the first time, I am just me—not somebody's daughter or wife or mother. I answer to me."

If you are a widow or widower, have you looked at your situation in that light? You have a new opportunity. You can remarry and continue habits that made your first spouse happy or you can rethink and do differently.

Try for a new job without having to think about how it affects another person. Do something drastically and completely different, something that makes your old friends say, "He's gone off his rocker," or causes them to secretly whisper, "I wish I had the nerve to do that."

Perhaps for the first time in your life you don't have to explain, forgive or correct. You can even dream old dreams in a fresh way. This is your chance to be yourself.

When the Philistines threaten to overwhelm you, remember that God is ready and willing to go to battle with you.

PRAYER: Heavenly Father, help me to face my Philistines in my own way, listening to the advice of others but making my own decisions according to Your guidance.

21

FROM

ASHES

READ: Isaiah 61

To give unto them beauty for ashes, the oil of joy for mourning, the garment of praise for the spirit of heaviness (Isaiah 61:3).

The death of a mate is never easy. Perhaps it is even more painful when that death arrives at the person's prime of life. It always dampens our joy, and sometimes it undermines our physical and mental health.

Death at the prime of life happened to Clint's wife. He picked up his telephone at work just as he'd locked his desk. The voice at the other end said, "There's been an accident. Your wife is dead and your daughter and son-in-law are in serious condition in the St. Charles hospital."

After the funeral, Clint decided to ask God to direct his future. God did.

One of Clint's coworkers introduced him to a career woman who would have been dubbed an "old maid" in days gone by. Clint was attracted to this short woman with the dark eyes, brown hair and dimples. Eventually they fell in love, married and ended up sharing many happy years together. The Lord turned Clint's mourning into the oil of joy.

The death of Deidre's husband was more expected. A visit to the doctor had resulted in a diagnosis of lung cancer and a verdict of "six months at the most." It was still a shock, though, when a few weeks before Christmas the time arrived.

Ever since Deidre's marriage twenty years before, she had written a verse for their Christmas cards, illustrated them and had them printed. This time it was so soon after her husband's death that she didn't feel up to it.

One day, while sorting out pictures she had decided to distribute to friends and relatives, she found one she'd forgotten she had. It was a photograph her husband had taken one day when the new snow had encrusted one side of the tree trunks. Two male cardinals brightened the limbs of one of the foreground trees. It looked like a Christmas scene, and she wondered if she could use that this year instead of making a new illustration. But where was the negative?

She searched through a number of films, holding many of them up to the light. Suddenly, she uttered a squeal of delight. She'd found it.

The Christmas card that year bore a bit of both of them, for the last time. She discovered there could be joy even in mourning.

These two individuals, Clint and Deidre, each managed, with God's help, to overcome mourning and continue in happiness of life.

PRAYER: Father God, help me to see that even in the darkest of times You are there and You care about me.

22

WHAT'S
IN A
NAME?

READ: 1 Chronicles 4:9,10

Surely goodness and mercy shall follow me . . . and I will dwell in the house of the LORD for ever (Psalm 23:6).

A lady who lives in a retirement complex was overheard to say, "I wish I'd decided to use my middle name when I moved here. It's so much easier than explaining my first."

Names can change. The apostle Simon's did. He became Peter. If you don't like yours, when you are leaving a job or moving to a different locale, why not modify it?

The son who was given the name of his father was often dubbed "Junior" as a boy. These men usually use their first name later on in life. A friend is still Theresa to me though her young friends call her Terry. One woman named Margaret always knows when her family calls—they ask for Margie.

One day some long-time, out-of-town friends

of mine visited my church. Since I was singing in the choir, they sat alone. They stood as visitors were introduced and when asked if they were visiting someone, the husband replied, "Maxine Dowd." I'll never forget the minister's reply: "You must be old friends of hers since we know her as Maxine Jensen."

Names had special meanings in Bible days. Jabez must have known his name meant "causing pain." His mother probably had a reason for that. She may have resented the misery she suffered at his birth and wanted the world to know. Jabez rose above this, though, and surely God rejoiced when He heard this man ask for blessing, enlargement and God's hand to keep him from evil.

God knows our true names. Maybe your parents called you "stupid," "dummy" or "clumsy," and perhaps this has hindered your belief in yourself. Maybe the world has labeled you a "street walker," a "drunken sot" or an "addict." By God's grace and your desire, these names can become obsolete.

If you would like to see a difference for good and for God in your life, ask Jesus Christ, the Savior of the world, to forgive you and to change you. Believe that God answers and rise to bear a new name—that of "Christian."

PRAYER: Oh, Lord, hear my prayer; change my name. As I live my life may I find Your hand upon me, leading me and keeping me from evil. May goodness and mercy follow me all the rest of my days.

23

READ

IT ALL

READ: Philippians

Rejoice in the Lord always and again I say rejoice (Philippians 4:4).

G o ahead. Read the whole thing. Philippians is a short book.

How do you feel today? Are you grumpy? Worried? Maybe it's time to do your income tax or some other equally forbidding task.

Perhaps you started out this way today, but trust me, reading the whole book of Philippians should put you in a better mood. Did you notice how many times *joy* and *rejoice* were used? Do you know that there is a difference between being happy and being filled with joy?

The American Heritage Dictionary defines happy as "characterized by good luck, fortunate." This indicates we need some tangible thing to make us happy, e.g., winning a lottery, being promoted, receiving a gift, having a child succeed in something. These are the things that make most people happy — especially if the good luck is unexpected.

Joy is different.

Joy is "a condition or feeling of great pleasure or happiness." Therefore, it doesn't depend on *receiving* something. Instead it's a condition or a "state of readiness." It's something inside that never really leaves us. It's having God's glasses on our eyes so we can "in everything" find a tidbit about which we can rejoice. Even with the IRS, we can be glad most of us don't have to contend with income tax but once a year.

The most important source of deep joy is the knowledge that when you know Jesus Christ as your Savior, there's been a good work begun in you that the Lord intends to continue in you until His return.

Another cause for rejoicing is that all our needs can be met. *In everything*, God's Word says, we can pour out our requests and our needs, and be thankful that our words, spoken or unspoken, are heard.

We can possess joy if we desire it. The fruits of righteousness are ours for the taking. Even Adam and Eve could have eaten of the Tree of Life.

Paul had confidence, something some of us lack or which flees from us in certain situations. However, we can possess it in Christ, increasing our joy.

Even when what we want is withheld, we can be joyful realizing God must have a better way. For instance, now that you are approaching or are already retired, perhaps you'd like to move. You pray and you put the "For Sale" sign on your lawn. Nothing happens. Instead of fuming and worrying, you can relax. In joy you can thank God. This may not be the Lord's time. God moves in mysterious ways, but He moves.

Joy is your right in Christ. It is not just a privilege which will ebb and flow. It can be a constant in your life if you will let it.

PRAYER: Wonderful Savior, thank You for planting joy in my heart. May it grow within me so that "in everything" I can see Your moving power and rejoice evermore.

24

MIDLIFE

CRISIS

READ: 2 Samuel 11:1-27

Be on your guard; stand firm in the faith; be men of courage; be strong. Do everything in love
(1 Corinthians 16:13,14, NIV).

David stayed home from the war; he slept with Bathsheba; he put out a contract on Uriah. Had midlife crisis struck him?

Has midlife crisis struck you?

This crisis seems to happen more often to men than to women, and evangelist Billy Graham addressed it in a recent column, saying, "It brings special temptations . . . temptations to leave the past [spouse and children] . . . and to seek adventure in some radically different [and sometimes wrong] way."

At this crossroad in life is it possible to find yourself at a standstill? Things are okay—in a way. You know your work, but it's become boring. You watch younger employees climb ladders to better jobs while you rest on a plateau.

Marriage has lost its excitement; you take

each other for granted. You notice the crow's feet at your wife's eyes or your husband's hairbrush contains more hairs than before and some of them are white.

You become restless, unhappy with the status quo. What can you do about it?

Many men desire a younger woman, but that's really the coward's way out. A young woman may make you feel youthful for awhile but it could be a real chore to keep up with her. And do you really want to throw away your life's investment in the woman you've chosen to love and marry? As for your job, it's probably unwise to walk away from that and throw away your seniority and your security if you have no other plans or skills.

There has to be a better way, and there is.

Job situations can be changed without necessarily involving a move to another company. Is there a routine operation that you could try another way, getting the same result but maybe saving time or introducing some variety? Do you handle some things in which you can expand the parameters? Can you think of a new idea that would add to and enhance what you do? Would going to a night school class (sometimes paid for by a company) teach you a new phase of your business that would broaden your promotion possibilities?

You can look for opportunities to change your marriage, too. Do you have a devotional time with your wife at breakfast or before retiring? Do you kiss her and tell her, each night, that you love her? Women like to hear the words. These three tiny words, sincerely spoken, may bear fruit in the way she talks to you and in what she does for you.

Have you gone on a vacation or a weekend getaway lately? When you do go on vacation, is your wife still encumbered with housekeeping and cooking chores? If so, why not choose a place where you can eat out, at least for your main meal? Do you vary your plans or discuss what you both would like to do? Maybe this area could use a compromise — one year her selected spot, the next yours.

Do you really listen to her or have you turned her off because she's always talking? This situation, too, can be repaired if you really listen and respond.

Do you favorably comment on her appearance when she looks attractive? Anybody — child, adult, male or female — glows at a sincere compliment. It makes that person feel good. He or she remembers your thought and often tries to do something nice for you in return.

Remember your courtship. Bring back some of the things you did then but which, for one reason or another, have slipped away. Try opening the car door for her, or leaving the light on in the garage so she can see more clearly as she walks to the back door. Little things mean a lot, especially to a woman.

Some men rush into an affair or a divorce and then hate to admit it was a mistake. Are you man enough to see, recognize and correct your errors? David was.

We are human. We fall once in a while. Yet God is a forgiving Lord, and if we seek Him before we make our decisions, He can give us the wisdom to know what's right and the strength to do it. He'll also show us the way out of the pitfall we so easily fall into.

You can change a possible midlife crisis into a lifelong victory.

PRAYER: Oh Lord, sometimes I'm weak. Help me to be strong. Often I need wisdom. Give it to me, I pray. Be with me and help me solve my problems and avoid the pitfalls of life wherever possible.

25

ALONE
BUT NOT
LONELY

READ: 1 Kings 19:8-18

Be content with such things as ye have: for he hath said, I will never leave thee, nor forsake thee (Hebrews 13:5b).

The American ideal of being independent, free-spirited and untethered by commitments makes for great drama but not necessarily for a great life. It's been said that twenty-one million Americans live by themselves, and of the people who are older than sixty-five, half are included in that number. However, many of these are not *lonely*.

Lonesomeness is different from loneliness. The former is usually temporary; the latter, if you let it, can be permanent and ruin your life. If you have a constant empty feeling for at least a year, you may be wise to seek help from a counselor.

Loneliness can be social or emotional. The first, social separateness, usually results from physical isolation. Elderly people often fit into this category. The second, emotional withdrawal, stems from a lack of close ties. If a mate is distant or cold, this supposed "close tie" can bring on feelings of emptiness even when you're still with the other person.

Divorce, being part of a single-parent family and the increased mobility of our society can affect your sense of belonging. Most widows will tell you that being the remaining partner of a couple causes a certain amount of isolation and different treatment by other people.

Many people wear a facade. Until you extend a hand of friendliness toward them, you may never know that they hurt and are as lonely as you may feel.

Here are some ideas for you to help relieve your sense of loneliness:

Look up an old friend. Mend some fences between yourself and your relatives. Treat yourself to a concert, an aerobics class or a night school course. The individual beside you may also need a new friend.

Get out of the house. Do something not just for yourself but for someone else. Join a group that is singing or learning to paint, to carve, to cook. Becoming part of a Bible study class or dieting with someone else can dispel your vacant feeling.

Don't forget, the Lord is waiting to become your nearest and dearest friend.

In youth groups and camp meetings of the past, a chorus we often sang had words that went something like this:

No, never alone; no, never alone;
He's promised never to leave me,
Never to leave me alone.

No matter how lonely you feel, Jesus is right at your elbow. Reach out and touch Him when you're feeling low.

PRAYER: Dear Friend and Savior, being alone often causes me to feel lonely. Help me not to let this loneliness become an integral part of my life, but let it be just a temporary bypass. Make me to know I shall return from these moments as I reach out to others and to You.

26

LAY OUT

THE FLEECE

READ: Judges 6:34-40

Get up, go down against the camp, because I am going to give it into your hands (Judges 7:9*b*, NIV).

When my father fell ill, I became the breadwinner in my family. Resentment of my situation never entered my consciousness, though. Perhaps this was because I was an only child and there was no one else to do it.

Years later the death of my mother ended my responsibilities and I asked God for guidance. At last I could do whatever He wanted or go wherever He chose to lead me. This was important to me because before I had acquired my responsibilities, I had considered becoming a missionary. I realized all I needed was health and a little money – and I had both. Age thirty-eight wasn't too late to change directions. In fact, I felt it could be the perfect time.

I had relied on God all my life, and He'd never failed, so I again asked for His guidance. The only option I didn't offer God was marriage.

Though I'd never been domestically inclined,

I'd never lacked dates. However, when the men I dated began to look, act or talk seriously, I ran.

Imagine my consternation when, through unusual circumstances, I met Cliff and realized this man was the kind I had dreamt about since my teen years. But still, I wondered if it wouldn't be wise to run again. I felt marriage was the biggest gamble of a person's life.

I'd never had it so good now that I was on my own. Should I give up my freedom? I fought with myself—and with God.

This man was too good for me. I couldn't cook or clean the right way. What if I couldn't really love him? Yet this man drew me as had no other.

So I did what I've heard some people say is done by amateur Christians. (Personally, I never classified Gideon as an amateur God-lover.) I laid out the fleece. Three times. Time has erased an accurate memory of the things which I requested, but each time, God did for me what was possible but highly improbable. Eventually I surrendered, and this surrender led to some of the happiest years of my life.

Do you rebel at submission? If it's God's choice for you that you rebel at, you're foolish to agonize about it.

What are you concerned about today that may bring you unsurpassed happiness tomorrow? Bring it to the Lord. Lay it at His feet—be you man or woman—and trust God to show you His will.

PRAYER: God, increase my faith, show me Your way, and lead me in a right path.

SECTION III
DO UNTO OTHERS

27

HERE

AM I

READ: 1 Samuel 3:1-10

What shall we do, that we might work the works of God? (John 6:28)

Excitement need not fly out of your life just because you are no longer eighteen.

At eighteen, I experienced my first airplane and my first motorcycle rides. I thought the motorcycle far more thrilling. But that kick paled compared to another, years later.

In the summertime, my husband and I often watched auto races from the stands at the raceway oval in Blue Island, Illinois. We also turned on the television for the races at Indy and Daytona. So, when the mayor of Lincoln, Alabama, invited me to visit the Alabama International Motor Speedway and meet the manager, I accepted.

Was I surprised! TV doesn't begin to show the vastness of these major tracks. The one in Alabama is even a bit larger and slightly longer than Indy or Daytona. As I stood high above the lanes, its immensity awed me.

"Would you like a ride in the official pace car?" the manager asked. We came down to the straightaway. The mayor climbed into the back seat and I sat in the front of a white car with psychedelic painting on the hood.

Our ride began slowly and sedately. Past the pits, down the lengthier part of the track, around the ends. I'm sure my mouth dropped open as I saw the steep sides at the oval's curves.

Automatically I reached for the bar on the dash before me. I think I stuttered as I asked, "Are we going up there?"

We did.

I saw bits of grass, flakes of billboards, slices of sky, cotton balls of cloud as we sped down the straight stretch, then onto the middle track on those 45 degree ends. My heart raced, too. My face glowed, I'm sure, and my knuckles on the dash bar grew white.

I never had a more exciting, exhilarating, too-short experience in my life. I know why drivers face injury and death to race again and again. This grey-haired grandma would do it, too. I proudly display the certificate indicating I've ridden at more than 100 miles per hour, and I almost stood on my head while doing it.

Your bonus years can be as exciting. Your driver is God. Underneath are the everlasting arms cradling you far more safely than a metal pace car.

What would your Lord like you to do for Him? Man a lifeline for an agency seeking to help the poor, the aged, the sin-chained individual? Spend time on a foreign mission field in 105° heat repairing a church? Are you a doctor, optometrist, nurse? Can you give your time to some needy part of the world?

Have you been an accountant, a teacher, a physical therapist, a farmer? Do you speak a foreign language, know how to fight agricultural pests? Can you sing a lullaby to a sick orphan as you cradle that child in your arms?

A missionary friend once described her feelings as the elephant she was riding slipped down the bank of a river. She nearly went over his head into that river. My reaction to the pace car ride dims beside the nerve-wracking ride she experienced.

A chaplain I knew had to run to the side of the road and vomit at his first glimpse of Dachau, the German prison camp, but he was able to return and minister to the people.

God has a place for you to show your love for Him and for mankind. Ask Him.

It might prove heart-rending or back-breaking. Could you do it? If you try, your face may glow with such a God-given light that those to whom you minister will be encouraged. Those who hear of you and see the light of God shining in your eyes may decide themselves to say to God, "Here am I." Age will not be a deterrent.

PRAYER: Lord, I seem to find excuses some Sundays for not even walking a few blocks to church. Challenge me. Give me a willing heart so I, too, will say, "Here am I."

28

THE FRAGRANCE OF YOU

READ: Ephesians 5:1,2,8-10,19,20

See that you walk . . . redeeming the time
(Ephesians 5:15,16a).

I once wrote an article that I knew was good but it was constantly rejected. As I looked at it more closely on its thirty-second return, I realized the title was too negative: "The 'Nothing' Talents." I retitled it "The Fragrance of You" and it sold the next time out. The focus had been shifted and, in fact, the article has now appeared a number of times in both religious and secular publications.

Perhaps, now that you are approaching or are in retirement, you need to change the focus of your life or at least take some minor steps in that direction.

You can start with some simple, thoughtful measures of kindness like these:

Jean's husband went for tests to a hospital within walking distance of their home. Winter's

86

blasts were spine-chilling that year, and Jean had never learned to drive.

Her friend Marlys had retired early to spend the last few months with her dying husband. After his death, she had many free hours. Marlys drove Jean to the hospital every day of Jean's husband's tests and after his operation.

Marlys and her husband had been good friends with Jean and her husband, but Jean couldn't believe Marlys would give up this much time for them. Jean praised Marlys to the point of almost canonizing her.

People in small towns often have to travel to larger ones for complex surgery or for advanced treatments. Ruth could drive the 150 miles, but how grateful she was every time one of her friends said, "When are you planning to visit Jim? May I drive you?"

Often, when Laura, a working woman, arrived home from visiting her hospitalized husband, her phone would ring. It would be her apartment neighbors, Mil or Bill, calling to say they had leftovers from their dinner keeping warm in their oven. "Will you come down or shall one of us bring them up?" It's nice to come home and not have to fix a meal at a time when even the thought of cooking is exhausting.

What do you do when illness comes to a friend or neighbor? What can you do for them? Are you willing to show you care and, therefore, leave a bit of your fragrance with another person?

PRAYER: Dear God, little things are sometimes more appreciated when they come from a friend to a friend. Help me not to hesitate if more is needed. Help me remember that a call, a card or a tiny piece of myself is always welcome in any time of need.

29

THE
1990s

READ: Matthew 28:18-20

The King will reply, "I tell you the truth, whatever you did for one of the least of these brothers of mine, you did it for me" (Matthew 25:40, NIV).

A few of the prophets for the 1990s drew a sketch of life in this decade that looks similar to what some of us will remember from the '50s. A trend analyst in New York says, "We're going to see a redirection of priorities, more toward human needs, as everyone ages." Hallelujah! The '70s were certainly the "Me, myself and I" decade, and the '80s password was "greed."

An assistant professor of business administration at Georgetown University sees women wanting "blue skies . . . clean air . . . and white water" rather than power. An author forecasts we'll take walks, climb mountains and listen to the sounds of nature.

Does this seem too Edenic for our present world? Will we finally be coming to our senses, rediscovering the joys of the Lord's creation, and putting some God-given compassion to work for our fellowman?

Vivian has been doing this ever since her husband died. In a letter I received this week, she tells me she's just returned from a trip to Brazil with a work team. "While we were there we completed the shell of the building for the congregation at San Jose Rio Preto, Sao Paulo," she said.

The countryside there is like Pennsylvania but the temperature was 105°. They lived in the homes of church members. This was different from her two work trips to Costa Rica where they stayed at a mission house.

Her letter glowed with God's perfect timing. The steady rain of a three-week period let up upon their arrival. It returned the evening of the day of the concrete pouring. This was exactly the right moment to begin the "seasoning" of the concrete.

Have you a desire to see foreign lands, listen to a different tongue, taste more than hamburgers and serve your God at the same time? My friend has discovered an interesting way to do all of this. You can, too.

Your bonus years are when God intends you to be free to investigate, not vegetate. Change is a challenge. It's also a way to prove you are young at heart though your hair may be tipped with silver and your knees occasionally creak.

PRAYER: Lord, lead me. Use me for Your glory.

30

GOD BLESS

THE VOLUNTEERS

READ: Matthew 7:1-12

Whatsoever ye would that men should do to you, do ye even so to them (Matthew 7:12a).

Those people past fifty make up the largest number of volunteers in small towns. In fact, Mountain Home, Arkansas, would be at a loss if all those helpers who are past seventy stopped working. Hundreds of jobs would go undone. Yes, they are little things like passing out menus to hospital patients, filling water carafes at bedside tables, and writing letters to a stroke victim's family, but they are important. And they make a difference in the lives of others.

In a small town, finding ways to serve your community by volunteering are more easily tracked down than in big cities. But any time expended looking for the opportunity that fits you will be greatly rewarded.

A recent Kansas City paper caption read, "Want to help? You can volunteer." It listed seven possible opportunities, which included many talents and some even provided special training:

Leaders — for support groups.

Sales clerks and clerical assistants — for a hospital.

Entertainers — for non-profit organizations, senior citizens' groups and children's centers.

Speakers — to discuss domestic violence before church and civic organizations (training provided).

Child care providers.

Drivers — to deliver meals, two hours, one day a week.

Retired teachers — to share experiences with college students who are preparing for education careers in inner-city schools.

Would any of the above appeal to you? Could you do these things in your community? For a Christian, these opportunities are not just to do something helpful but they also hold the chance of giving words of encouragement or of sharing spiritual happenings in your life.

Art had an unobtrusive, fascinating way of turning a conversation with a waiter, a sales clerk or a receptionist into a talk about God. Probably after the discussion the person wondered, *How did we ever get on that subject?* Since it was amicably presented, no argument ever arose and no trouble ever resulted, but people were motivated to think. Who knows how many people Art helped and is still helping?

Eleanor Roosevelt once wrote in her column not to bother God with little things. My Sunday school teacher said in contrast, "The Lord is interested in *everything* about us." I put the almighty to the test one morning on my way to school.

At age eight, I'd been jumped by a German shepherd whose owner caught him at the last fearful moment. Thus began my dread of dogs. I was twelve and tiny when I entered high school. Every day on my mile-and-a-half walk to school, I met at least one dog. I crossed the street, I slowed down, I walked faster – and still they yapped at my heels.

One day, after hearing my Sunday school teacher's comment, I saw a dog up ahead. Brash me decided to test the almighty. I said something like, "If You answer prayer, God, and if you really are interested in *everything* about me, don't let that dog pay any attention to me." I walked straight ahead. The dog continued to sniff something and didn't even look at me.

I floated on a cloud the rest of the way to school. I discovered my Sunday school teacher was right and the wife of the President of the United States was wrong.

You can pray for guidance in helping others. Examine your own unique talents, and let God lead you to the volunteer work where you can be effective and bring praise to His name.

PRAYER: God, sometimes I feel I have no talents. Forgive me because I know I must possess at least one. Show me what it is, give me a willing spirit to use it, and lead me to the right place where I can serve as You would have me to.

31

FISHING
FOR FISH
OR MEN?

READ: Mark 1:14-20

"Come, follow me," Jesus said, "and I will make you fishers of men" (Mark 1:17, NIV).

Joe looked forward to moving to sunny shores and a good-looking retirement village. "I'll be able to fish and play golf anytime and as often I want," he told himself. One day, though, Joe's wife found him humped over in his big living room chair, his chin in his hands and a frown on his brow.

"What's wrong, Joe?" she asked.

"Retirement isn't what it's cracked up to be."

Joe and his wife began attending a small church in a nearby town. It was a little church where most of the couples were young with children. Joe's eyes began to twinkle when he stopped to talk to some of the lads, and soon he asked the church school superintendent if he could teach a class. His first lesson was about the fisherman Peter.

Hardly realizing what he was doing, he asked the boys in his class, "Would you like to go fishing?" Before long he was teaching them, and other boys, how to fish and tie flies and how to make fly books in which to carry these lures. Life took on new meaning for him, and his Christian beliefs and principles were finding lodging in the hearts of *his* boys.

Would you like to be a fisher of men? Check the rescue missions in your area. They usually welcome help and it will give you a chance to spread the word for Jesus. Visitation assignments for your local church are also a good opportunity. You will make new friends and you can share the good news of Jesus with others.

Use your bonus years to look for new ways to share the gospel with those around you.

PRAYER: Father, make me a fisher of men in my future years.

32
THE GIFT
OF LITERACY

READ: 1 Timothy 4:13-16

Till I come, give attendance to reading
(1 Timothy 4:13a).

When I read in our local paper, "The Literacy Council of Cass County will sponsor training sessions next month for volunteers who want to teach people to read," I thought of Fay. She is retired and this is one of her activities. She belongs to the Literacy Volunteers of America.

Not to be able to read—think of that. It hampers an individual in the working world. And think of how much that person misses recreationally and psychologically.

A book can allow you to forget your problems—for the moment at least—and transport you into a different world. It may be a world of make-believe or a new area of learning.

Fay has been teaching English as a second language. This means she, too, is learning—learning new customs and new ways of using words. Last year she taught a Puerto Rican lady.

This year she teaches a Vietnamese man. Both began at about the third-grade level and progressed to fifth. The man needs more assistance in speaking English but he is grasping the reading of it.

Some students go on to pass the GED exam and receive a high school diploma; others feel they do not need to advance that far. Many are hoping to be able to get better jobs by learning more. And there are parents who would like to be able to read to their children.

If you like reading, would you be willing to open this door to another person? It takes no more of your time than you wish to give. Fay donates an hour a week. The materials are usually provided by the literacy program.

If you are in business for yourself and cannot spare the time at the moment, you may have employees who could profit from these teachings. You could support such an effort for your workers.

If becoming a literacy tutor is something you're interested in knowing more about, contact your local public library. If no program exists in your area, write to one of these organizations for more information:

Literacy Volunteers of America
5795 Widewaters Parkway
Syracuse, NY 13214

Christian Literacy Associates
541 Perry Highway
Pittsburgh, PA 15229

You can give an adult the gift of literacy.

PRAYER: Lord, reading has given me so much pleasure and so much knowledge, and it has helped me learn so much more about You. Help me to give back some of what has been given to me.

33

CARRY FOOD
TO THE
HUNGRY

READ: Luke 9:10-17

He saith unto them, Give ye them to eat . . . And they did eat, and were all filled (Luke 9:13a,17a).

Fay and Jerry retired in a little town in Michigan. Most of their volunteer work in Chicago had been connected with their church: serving on committees, singing in the choir and being active in various men's and women's groups.

However, retirement gave them a lot more time. In addition to working in their new church, they decided to broaden their volunteerism. They are now active in the Meals on Wheels program, delivering meals to house-bound people. Through their visits they have made many new friends and encouraged people whose shut-in situations often lead to loneliness.

One day there was a new name at the bottom of the list of houses to visit. The location lay a bit beyond the city limits and the day couldn't make up its mind whether to rain, sleet or snow. Jerry sighed as he left his usual last stop.

He climbed the steps at the new place and stomped his feet as he waited for the door to open. The lady who greeted him used a walker.

"Won't you come in and visit while I eat?" she asked. "I've a full coffee pot on the stove."

Jerry didn't answer for a moment. It was his last stop and with the weather worsening, it would be good to get home. Out of the corner of his eye, though, he saw a piano. Immediately he replied, "I'll be glad to."

Once inside, his coat and boots shed, he asked, "Could I try your piano?"

"Please do," she answered as she filled the coffee cups.

Jerry loved music and as he played, he sang in his strong bass voice, his coffee forgotten.

"My son used to play and sing," the woman said as he prepared to leave. "He was killed in Vietnam."

Somehow both Jerry's body and heart were warm as he drove back home.

Many organizations, like the Pacific Garden Mission in Chicago, Catholic churches and the Salvation Army, serve meals to indigent street people. These groups hold Christ high and can often use interested, concerned helpers. In these places there are often opportunities to pray for and with these needy people.

Retirement can be a time when your own

heart softens toward the less fortunate and when God can lead you into wider paths of service.

PRAYER: Lord God, help me to seek and find new avenues of service to fill my hours of freedom.

34

A
LITTLE
TOOLBOX

READ: Galatians 6:1-5

Let us not be weary in well doing for in due season we shall reap, if we faint not (Galatians 6:9).

Chris always carried a toolbox with him. A white-collar worker by day, he became a blue-collar worker by night.

His wife had many single women friends and some of them supported their widowed mothers. When visiting these friends, Chris would notice a porch step that hung by one nail, a toaster that didn't pop up as intended, a refrigerator that failed to close properly. First he would ask, then, when he received an affirmative reply, he would proceed to fix the problem. He and his wife were always welcome in these homes.

After he retired he continued to keep everything functioning in his own home and he helped his wife's friends when they needed him. He played golf and he went fishing, but these things didn't keep him busy enough.

One day he asked his pastor for the names of some of the poorer families in the congregation. He made it his personal responsibility to visit these people and, while there, he kept his eyes open. When he saw things that needed fixing, he again asked permission and then fixed them.

Maybe you're not a handyman, but what talent do you possess? What skills have you developed? Can you put them to use for your church, for people who are less fortunate than yourself, for friends? It could be an excellent use of your time both before you retire and after.

PRAYER: God lead me to a need I can care for that Your name may have the glory.

35

HELP
IN A
HOSPICE

READ: Isaiah 61:1-3

Bind up the brokenhearted (Isaiah 61:1*b*).

About ten years ago, a doctor in Mountain Home, Arkansas, began a health-care program for terminally ill, needy people. This developed into Hospice of the Ozarks.

Originally, people with cancer, strokes or various other physical conditions could use the services. However, because of the growth of the area and the increased need, it became necessary to limit the program to help for cancer patients only.

My husband had died of cancer, so when a program was being designed for those who'd been widowed, I volunteered. I attended a training seminar on how to help both the ill and the bereaved.

Like a number of other volunteers, I would take these people to medical appointments or to beauty parlors, or I'd pick up drug-store items and groceries, or help them with other necessary tasks.

Sometimes after I'd visited a home several times, I would learn the patient had difficulty eating, so I would suggest his wife use a blender for things like beef stew. My husband had said, "I agree it doesn't look as appetizing, but the flavor is the same." I would also take a bottle of Tang and a package of instant breakfast with me when I visited the next time. Tang and the instant breakfast mix had helped sustain my husband during his last days.

As you get to know the patient and the family, you may find openings to share about the Lord and His compassion and comfort. I've found it important to be sensitive to the patient's needs and his willingness to discuss spiritual matters.

The saddest part of involvement in this program is the death of the patient. Often, the family wants you, the hospice volunteer, to be with them at that moment or soon afterward. You can put your arms around them, pat them as you would a baby, and let them cry on your shoulder. You needn't say anything. The fact that you are there and that you care is enough. You'll be surprised at how your heart will sing when you've been of help to a grieving individual or family.

Becoming a hospice volunteer is not for everyone. But if you feel the Lord has led you in this direction and you have a tender heart and servant spirit, there are many families in need of your caring attitude.

PRAYER: Father God, help me to realize that my joy can arise when I comfort someone who feels all meaning in life is gone.

36

A

MAJORITY

OF ONE

READ: Nehemiah 4:1-9,14,15 and 6:1-3,15,16

I can do all things through Christ which strengtheneth me (Philippians 4:13).

God's math doesn't work as ours does. An army of men slay more than their own entire number and capture the balance of the enemy's army; five loaves and two fish feed a multitude; five stones and one little boy defeat a giant. As you read the Bible, especially the Old Testament, notice how often a handful of God's people accomplish amazing changes. You can be this type of individual.

Years ago, diminutive Mary Slessor wanted a Sunday school class. Told she'd have to recruit her own, she went out into the streets to do so. The leader of a gang of boys deliberately tested her by swinging a sling shot ever nearer to her forehead. She didn't flinch and he dropped his weapon and told his gang to follow her. She made a difference in their lives. When Mary journeyed to Africa as a missionary, she brought Christ to the natives and often sat in their tribal meetings, helping to settle their disputes.

These "miracles" are still happening today.

One woman's vote against her own church uniting with a neighboring church kept this from happening and proved to be the turning point in the ultimate resurrection of a failing congregation.

Modern Maturity, in its February-March 1990 issue, tells of Ed Cooper who "built an oasis" in a trash-strewn urban neighborhood. Today he is co-founder and president of Boston Urban Gardeners. The result is 120 gardens in low-income, multicultural areas. These gardens are now supported by city officials and residents of all ages.

He has further plans which include educating public school students. He wants to interest them in beautifying their surroundings and make them aware of the need for gardening to provide food for others.

Have you ever heard someone say that one person can't make a difference? It's simply not true.

What would you like to accomplish or change? How would you like to make a difference in someone's life? Remember you are a majority of one. Add God's power and sanction, and you can move a mountain.

PRAYER: Dear Lord, sometimes I feel insignificant and helpless to change things or to really make a difference. Give me wisdom. Give me courage. Give me Your cooperation.

SECTION IV
HOME IS
WHERE THE
HEART IS

37

HOSPITALITY
AT HOME

READ: Luke 6:46-49

As Jesus and his disciples were on their way, he came to a village where a woman named Martha opened her home to him (Luke 10:38, NIV).

Your house tells a lot about you. There may be more people viewing it when you retire. What will it say?

One large house I have visited has two beautiful fireplaces. They reach at least twenty-five feet above the floor in both the living room and the family room. However, the size of these rooms and the height of the ceilings reveal that any heat engendered by these beauties would be like a lone glowing coal on an ice field.

The family room has plump pillowed sofas and potted plants throughout but not a single lamp on even one table. A sparkling chandelier hangs from the ceiling over the dining room table and the crystal candelabrum on the table gleams. Four chairs surround the five-foot round glass top.

You can often tell what kind of people the

owners are by the home in which they live. What would this house tell you?

Once a friend said to me, "You have books in every room." Yes, every room except the bathrooms. And that tells you something about me.

In our bonus years, including warmth, illumination and hospitality in our lives keeps us from growing old. It's important especially if we wish to have friends and continue the good work our Lord has begun in us.

Hospitality is a mark of the Christian. Remember those who opened their homes to Paul and the other early Christians? Hospitality is never out-of-date and it will enhance your life. Keep your home and your heart open to others.

We can share our warmth in other ways as well. We smile at acquaintances but do we look down at a child and do the same? Do we greet a stranger with a happy face? Do we reach out a hand to clasp another?

A smile can start a friendship, lift the heart of a passerby, begin a love affair in the soul of a child.

In each neighborhood where I lived I was either able to walk to work or walk to the public transportation provided a few blocks from my home. I met various elderly ladies coming from mass as I briskly went my way. I smiled. Soon we said something and then we became friends. I always missed them whenever I moved.

Retirees and those over fifty-five seeking a healthy, agile body often walk or run. How about a smile as you pass someone? You will leave a fragrance behind that indicates to others you are a warm-hearted person.

Often the warmth and happiness you exude will lead to illumination. It begins to tell the story of what makes you the kind of person you are.

When I was young, I thought witnessing meant telling someone he or she was a sinner and needed a Savior. I know I would have rebelled if someone had approached me in this manner. As I mature, I realize I can testify in other ways. I can show Christ's love when I'm kind to a stranger. I share His compassion when I help a sick friend. I try to speak of my God-given blessings and my answers to prayers to others. I feel these bring the light of the gospel to those with whom I visit.

Think of ways you can impart the love of Christ in your life to others.

PRAYER: Dear Lord, remind me to use my hospitality, my warmth and my smile to share my love for you. I want others to be pointed to You because of me.

38

THE

GREAT

OUTDOORS

READ: Genesis 1

God saw all that he had made, and it was very good (Genesis 1:31*a*).

Every year since 1975, one of my pieces, "My Snow Prayer," has sold to at least one additional publication. The writing of it came about because of my love of birds.

The day before a five-inch snow fell, I bought bird seed and filled my feeders. The next morning my deck was covered not only with whiteness but also with a congregation of happy birds.

I sat at my dining room table and watched a scarlet cardinal dip his wing in greeting. I noticed the snow birds were dressed for this first winter banquet in black tie and tails. The melodious, colorful meadowlarks were eating the fallen crumbs from the porch deck. A neighbor hardly believed the latter because, she said, meadowlarks only eat from the ground. On this day, however, and on some future days, they managed to flit five feet up to my deck.

My heart sang with joy at the sight and I wrote my popular piece that morning.

In my bonus years, I find I have some time really to enjoy God's wonderful world. Birds are some of His most beautiful creations. I understand a bird sanctuary near or in South Africa is host to nearly every species known to man. I'd like to visit it some day.

Birds caused a friend who was dying of cancer to glow. She looked out her hospital window each day and watched the birds gather around a feeder the hospital administrator had ordered be put up. They brought her joy.

Watching birds can be as interesting as watching people. Did you know that hummingbirds have different personalities? A mockingbird used to greet me each time I stepped out on our deck. He did trampoline work on the telephone pole at the corner of our lot while trilling his melodies. I called him "prima donna." I was so ignorant when I moved there—I didn't realize it's the male who sings.

If you want to enjoy birds around your present or future home, you can lure them there. Some plantings which entice the most of these creatures are:

Autumn Olive	25 species
Holly	22 species
Cherry	40 species
American Cranberry bush	34 species

Flowering Dogwood	36 species
Highbush Blueberry	36 species
Hawthorn	25 species
Red Cedar (a tree that grows to 40 feet)	68 species
Virginia Creeper	37 species

Many other bushes, like bittersweet, are also bird favorites.

Birdwatching is just one way to enjoy the beauty around us. Nothing will make you feel more alive than some moments spent appreciating what God has created. Think of a couple of ways you could enjoy nature this week.

PRAYER: Lord, how I love the sights and excitements of nature which You've provided for me. Help me to enjoy each day more because of these gifts.

39

"MOM, I'M HOME!"

READ: 2 Samuel 18:24-33

I laid me down and slept; I awaked: for the LORD sustained me (Psalm 3:5).

The words, "Mom, I'm home," issued from my mouth every time I stepped in our front door.

Today these words are heard in homes across America, but many times they come from the mouth of an adult child who is returning home after a broken marriage.

If you took a look at our society right now, you'd find that many grandparents are raising grandchildren and even great-grandchildren. Parents separate, divorce or die. They desert their children to pursue drugs. Some become parents before they are emotionally ready.

Albert and Mary hoped retirement would bring them relaxation, enjoyment and traveling. Instead, they are miserable and have little time for themselves. Rather than doting on their grandchildren, they are disciplining them.

For some, the feeling of guilt squeezes out

happiness. *Where did we go wrong in raising our children?* they ask themselves.

King David faced this situation with his son Absalom. He felt guilty because his son turned against him and everything he stood for. Yet when he fled because his son sought to destroy him, he slept (see Psalm 3).

Difficult situations can bring happiness when we believe that God's power can enable us to make our own joy. We, too, can sleep.

You may look at your grandchild and remember that once your daughter's or your son's eyes sparkled like this young child's do. These thoughts may depress you at first. But if you rejoice that these eyes of the little one *are* alive and pray that they may remain so, a sparkle will return to your own. A smile will steal across your features.

If you are caring for a grandchild, discuss with your mate the things you might have or wished you'd done differently. Realize that you've been given a second chance.

PRAYER: Dear Lord, although this isn't exactly what I had planned for the bonus years, help me look for the good in this situation. I sincerely thank You for this child you've brought into our lives.

40

LETTING

GO

READ: Proverbs 22:6

And the child grew and became strong; he was filled with wisdom, and the grace of God was upon him (Luke 2:40, NIV).

One day, a few years before my mother's death, I told her, "I want you to know I've appreciated something that is missing in the relationships of most of my friends and their mothers. Whenever I faced a big decision in my life, you electioneered for what you thought was the right path for me. Many times I did not follow your advice. My friends hear, 'I told you so,' or the subject is continually thrown up at them. Yet, once I decide, I never hear a word or see a disapproving expression on your face. I'm glad, but why are you different?"

She sat still for a moment before replying.

"You are the one who must live with your decision, and I know you pray before you make your choice. Plus," she smiled as she said the last words, "you always seem happier in the weeks that follow what *you've* chosen to do."

Every child or young adult needs a gradual loosening of the ties that can bind you too close. Permit these growing individuals to make decisions. Some of their choices may be against what you feel is best. However, in order to grow, we stumble once in a while. The important thing is to encourage your young person to pick himself or herself up and go forward—wiser and surer.

Caution your children, explain your reasons, love them, pray for them, and then let them make decisions of their own.

PRAYER: Oh, Lord, help me to know when to refrain from interfering in the lives of my children. Watch over them when I can't be there. Give me Your insight on relating to them as adults.

41

BELOVED

AND GREAT

PHYSICIAN

READ: Luke 8:43-48

The people . . . followed him: and he . . . healed them that had need of healing (Luke 9:11).

Scholars tell us that Luke had a good command of languages and an extensive and rich vocabulary. The latter, they say, is evidenced by his style, sometimes approaching the classical Greek and other times being more Semitic.

As we read his beautifully written Gospel, we also note that he was a compassionate physician especially concerned for women. His knowledge of their needs was great. In fact, Luke is sometimes called the beloved physician.

As we enter our bonus years, it's wise to find a knowledgeable, compassionate doctor so that his care, coupled with our reliance on God, can help us remain as healthy as possible.

One doctor of my acquaintance was such a man. He once asked a young woman who supported her elderly mother, "It's just you and your mother?" When she replied yes, he said, "Of course you'll have to settle the hospital bill before she is released, but as for me, you can pay me when it's convenient."

Another time he decided to risk an operation—actually three of them which he had observed in Germany—on a fourteen-year-old girl who needed them and was strong enough to withstand the trauma. His pay would be the experience which would enable him to use the techniques later to help a number of other patients.

On still another occasion, he told the accounting office of a hospital to hold his patient's bill each week until it could be picked up by the family rather than following their regular custom of leaving it on the patient's bedside table. He didn't want his patient to fret about the charges.

If a move is part of your retirement, pray for guidance as you search for new doctors, dentists and other professional people. Many magazines run articles on how to choose the right physician (see *Modern Maturity*, August/September 1989). Television commercials often mention lists of certain types of physicians which can be obtained by calling a 1-800 number.

Choose your doctor with care, and then relax under the watchful eye of the Great Physician.

PRAYER: Lord, as I approach my bonus years and perhaps move to a new area after retirement, lead me to the right physician and make my later years as healthy as possible.

42

THE WATER
OF LIFE

READ: Isaiah 44:3,4

The LORD shall guide thee continually, and satisfy thy soul in drought . . . and thou shalt be like a watered garden (Isaiah 58:11).

My mother, a farmer's daughter, loved flowers and plants and she nurtured them carefully. They all responded to her care. During one six-week hospital confinement, she often asked me, "Are you watering my plants?"

My answer was, "Of course," and that night I'd pour water on every one.

One day a young couple brought her a beautiful African violet. She asked me to take it home for safe-keeping. About the time she died, the plant lost all its blooms, but, as with the other plants, I continued to water it—when I thought about it.

Imagine my delight and surprise when I discovered its first new bud. Somehow, I felt God was telling me something through that bud. It lifted my spirits and urged me on.

We all desire good physical health and good

spiritual health but not all of us succeed in enjoying both. No one can tell us *all* the secrets of keeping these precious possessions, but we do know that water is essential to our physical body.

Water, at least eight glasses a day, is said to be the minimum amount that good health requires, and it will aid the proper functioning of our kidneys and bowels. A contact lens wearer is often cautioned to drink lots of water so the eyes will be lubricated. Some diet-conscious individuals have discovered drinking water helps them lose weight. Since our body's highest percentage of compounds is composed of liquids, these recommendations sound sensible.

Our spiritual health requires water as well — the water of the Word of God. Christians are subject to many of the world's hard ways, and sometimes it is easy to become weighed down with them. In such times, we need to remember the biblical words, "Cast your burden upon the Lord"; and, "Rest in the Lord." Yet isn't there something we can do instead of just waiting?

There certainly is.

God offers us the water of life. Have you accepted Christ? If so, do you regularly drink at His fountain, the Bible?

Death Valley lives up to its name because of a lack of water. My mother knew her plants needed water. Often when I call an avid gardener friend, she has been out rearranging her water hoses so her plants' thirst can be quenched.

Bible verses can quench your thirst, too. They can enable you to grow and help you bear fruit. You can blossom as did my mother's African violet.

PRAYER: Dear God, quench my thirst; guide me continually; and help me to blossom like a watered garden.

43

WHEN
THE BODY
FALLS APART

READ: Ecclesiastes 12:1-5

Then man comes to his eternal home and mourners go about the streets (Ecclesiastes 12:5b, NIV).

Ecclesiastes 12 is a mournful chapter. Anyone who knows this portion of Scripture may have remembered it if they read one of the late 1989 editions of the *U.S.A. Weekend*. Baby boomers were told they were entering "The Ache Age." One Illinois baby-boomer says he now reaches for Ben Gay after exercising while everyone else reaches for a cold drink.

Some—maybe you—in this age bracket say they feel better than ever. "Life begins at forty" is an adage true of these individuals.

In a survey taken by *U.S.A. Weekend*, 50 percent of the baby boomers said they exercise regularly. Those who are not this diligent believe they should be, and most of them find it depressing to view their bodies in a full-length mirror. Where do you fit?

The middle years are the age when bifocals become necessary for many, when balding is a factor, and when plaque coats the teeth and arteries. Exercisers find their bodies don't bounce back as quickly.

To many people, the worst part of the middle years are the sags and wrinkles. However, these may not be a factor of age as much as they are of lifestyle. Have you been an avid sunbather? A chain smoker?

Pam Wenndt, a physical therapist in Iowa, believes the problems we ascribe to aging are actually the result of a poor diet, lack of exercise and high stress levels.

Believe it or not, our spiritual life can suffer from what we could call aging as well, and that, too, may be the result of a poor diet, lack of exercise and high stress levels.

For example, do you take time before or at breakfast to make God's Word food? Can you say with Jeremiah, "I did eat them" (15:16)? Before you retire do you reach for the Lord in prayer? How many days this week did you pause to exercise your memory and recite a Scripture verse? Have you shared what God did for you yesterday with someone today? Did you use a Bible verse to lighten the load of a friend or to relieve stress and calm your own soul?

Let's face it: The aging process is unavoidable. But by paying some attention to how we live, what we eat and how much we exercise, we can slow the process down — both physically and spiritually.

PRAYER: Father God, help me each day to feed on Your Word for nourishment and to exercise my beliefs by speaking to someone about You. Give me the confidence to relax in Your undergirding arms.

44

PAID

IN ADVANCE

READ: Psalm 37:1-13, 23-25

God is able to make all grace abound to you, so that in all things at all times, having all that you need, you will abound in every good work
(2 Corinthians 9:8, NIV).

Forty-five is too old to have a child, Em thought. *If it's deformed, I hope they let it die.*

But "they" didn't allow the little girl to die, and year by year, Em saw Maria's smaller left side growing to catch up to her right side. When entry into school was nigh, no one would have guessed the golden-curled, almost black-eyed girl had ever been less than perfect.

Em knew she was stricter with Maria than other mothers who were twenty years younger, and they didn't fret as much as she did over measles and childhood squabbles. Nonetheless, many of the young mothers treated Em as an equal, and they became friends. They met at their children's school, at church and at the supermart. They shared pie and coffee in cozy kitchens.

Em's spirits plummeted when her husband, flanked by two sturdy men, was brought home from work. Maria, just eighteen then and planning on college in the fall, became the breadwinner. Yet Em never heard a word of complaint from this girl. She remembered the time, years before during the great depression, when Maria had leaned on her knee, looked up into her eyes, and said, "God will take care of us, Mother."

God had done so. He'd supplied every need during the nearly twenty years that followed Em's husband's death, too. Not many luxuries, but every need.

On Christmas Day, following Em's third operation and twenty-four hours before she would die, she looked up at Maria from her bed. "You've been so good to me. I'll make it up to you some day."

She noticed the dimples flirting in Maria's cheek, saw the smile, noted the twinkle in those almost black eyes and heard the words, "Mother, you don't owe me anything. You paid all this in advance."

God is like that. He paid for our redemption — in advance. He's promised us joy, *always*. Let's quit fretting and trust Him for the future.

PRAYER: Dear Lord, when bad times come, I fret. I wonder how we will make out. When serious sickness descends, I worry — about bills, about its duration, about possible death. Lord, lead me into still waters and restore my soul to peace and joy. Help me to remember that You've already taken care of everything for me.

45

WISE IN

WORLDLY WAYS

READ: 1 Kings 17:2-16

Your Father knows what you need before you ask him (Matthew 6:8*b*, NIV).

Psychologists tell us that the only traumatic happening which affects 100 percent of those involved is the death of a spouse. As we age, we need to be aware of the increased chance that this can happen to us.

Many widows and widowers look forward to seeing their mates again in heaven. However, this doesn't assuage the sorrow of the parting and the days following it. Adjustments must be made.

One of these changes is the handling of monetary assets. One woman began to teach her husband how to balance their checkbook when she thought she was dying. Perhaps you're a wife who doesn't know how to care for what is left. It's wise for both men and women to learn as much as possible about their financial state before death or divorce forces a parting.

Another basic thing you should know is your

131

spouse's work record. Pension rights are now vested. Keep a record of the employment: length, location, telephone number and position occupied. Yes, God supplies all our needs, but if you have moved around in your jobs, there may be some pension money being held for you. It may be deferred by a previous employer and it must usually be applied for by you when you reach age sixty-five. Update this information frequently. Employers move, mergers occur and so do bankruptcies. At sixty-five you may need extra money, and the work records you keep may be God's way of helping you locate money that belongs to you — His way of supplying your needs.

If you are of pension-receiving age when your spouse dies, you'll be glad you kept such a record. Get it out and begin contacting the various firms to determine your rights.

Many employers make some type of lump-sum payment upon death. Do not be hasty in determining what you should do with it. Often the money can be rolled over into an interest-bearing account where you can receive monthly payments for ten or fifteen years.

Mary was fifty-two when her husband died. She chose to take payments from her husband's life insurance policy over a ten-year period since at the end of that time she would be eligible for Social Security.

A few cautions: Don't tie up a large sum hurriedly in a long-term investment. Until you know exactly where you will live and work and what your monthly needs will be, wait. Listen to the advice of friends and relatives, yet, as Shakespeare said, listen "but reserve thy judgment." Perhaps your best advice will come from an impartial, financial adviser.

Whatever you decide to do, first take your problem to the Lord. No one is more concerned about your welfare nor loves you more. When you do this, you can look up and smile at the world.*

PRAYER: Lord, this is a hard place for me, but I am confident that, even as You have led my spouse through the valley of the shadow of death, You can bring me out into the sunshine of living.

---

* I'd like to recommend a book I've written titled *Beginning Again* (Baker Book House, 1985). If your mate is still living, you'll find a helpful addendum which can begin to prepare you for the future. If you are a widow or widower, I've written this book especially for you. Check with your local Christian bookstore.

46

REMARRIAGE?
EASE THE
TRANSITION

READ: Ecclesiastes 9:9-11

Can two walk together except they be agreed?
(Amos 3:3).

Though the young may find it difficult to believe, love and sexuality do not necessarily diminish with age. "To marry after the death of a mate is a compliment to the previous spouse," said Chris, who lost his forty-three-year-old wife in a car accident when he was forty-five. Barney had the same experience. Both married forty-year-old women. Vicky and Chuck have outlived two husbands and two wives each.

Death to your spouse can come at any time, but the majority die sometime after age forty. The sadness that comes with this parting does not depend on the number of years of the marriage. Love torn from you after only a few months can be life-shaking and can leave a void as large as if you'd been together many years.

If you remarry today, you have many options. Some wives retain their name, their apartment, their car. A few husbands suggest changes in living quarters; some wish everything to remain the same.

Before Chris remarried he asked Mary, an apartment dweller, if she'd like him to tear the wall down between the living room and dining room of the house and put a picture window in the living room. To the first suggestion she said yes. To the latter she said, "I'd rather have the picture window in the bedroom where we'll have a view of the flowers behind the house than to be the picture ourselves to those passing on the street."

Two years later they had new wall-to-wall carpet in the two joined rooms, new furniture in the living room, but no picture window there — it was in their bedroom.

When Edie and Barney married, they left everything exactly as it had been in his house. Vicky and Chuck joined all their possessions in a brand new house in a different town.

You can decide which will work the best for you.

Chris and Mary never knew each other until they were matchmade by a fellow worker four months before they married. Working in adjoining buildings made it possible to meet for coffee nearly every day. If they were not on a date, they were likely having a long telephone conversation. In that quarter of a year, they learned more about each other than most would find out in four years of courtship. Chris was enough like Mary's mother to have been her son. The congenial relationship Mary had with her mother carried over into the marriage.

Barney had known Edie only through his occasional association with her brother. However, this former high school teacher's immediate rapport with Barney's two boys became a big plus in their relationship.

Vicky was Catholic; Chuck was Protestant. Both loved the Lord, and they had known each other and their two former spouses for many years. They compromised. They go to mass either at 4 P.M. on Saturdays or early Sunday morning. Then they go to Chuck's 11 A.M. Sunday service, even if they've already attended mass that morning.

True, long association, different faiths and getting to know one another well doesn't always work. It didn't for Trudy and Jake. Jake had worked with Trudy's husband Carl and the two couples had moved to the same town in their retirement. Jake's wife died several years before Trudy's husband, and Trudy married Jake just a month or two after Carl died of a long illness.

But Trudy knew Jake in outside situations only; she didn't know how he acted within his own doors. Sadly, the marriage lasted just a year.

As we grow older most of us "mellow." We know what is important and what can be overlooked. It's also true that we don't really begin to know a person until after the knot is tied.

When at forty I married my widower, I could find only one habit he had which I'd have preferred absent. He smoked. On the good side was the fact that he never exuded a stale tobacco smell, his fingers were never yellow and he was not a chain smoker. I knew I could never nag him about it or try to change him. Marrying a man in the hopes of changing him is always a mistake.

Five years after our marriage, my husband succeeded in quitting smoking. One day I looked up at him, a twinkle of truth in my eye, and said, "What am I going to do now? You've given up the only thing I didn't like about you."

Compromise is a good word to bring to a second marriage. Know what things about the prospective mate are worth overlooking and which ones might tear the marriage apart. If you see one or more of the latter, remember what Shakespeare said: "The better part of valor is discretion."

PRAYER: Lord, if remarriage becomes a possibility for me, please grant me wisdom to know what to do. If the answer is yes, I ask for the ability to change myself, if necessary, yet love the individual enough that I won't try to change that person.

SECTION V

WHERE JESUS IS

'TIS HEAVEN

47

MY

LITTLE

CORNER

READ: John 14:1-6

I go to prepare a place for you (John 14:2*b*).

When I was a child, I loved Saturdays at our house. I'd dash to the kitchen only to have my mother shoo me back to put slippers on my feet and wrap a robe about myself. All morning long I hovered near, snitching a piece of emerald citron or twirling a dried apple ring on my chubby finger.

Soon my mother opened the oven door and plucked from the heat a pan of fragrant rolls with delicate yellow insides and a faint sweet taste. I'd grab one. Its warmth made tossing it between my hands necessary. Then I'd slip a fat pat of golden butter deep into its innards. As I smacked my lips and licked the melting butter running down my pudgy fingers, my mother would say, "You'll ruin your stomach eating that hot bread," but the twinkle in her eyes assured me she wouldn't stop me.

The Bible tells us that Christ is building many

mansions for us. I don't know if I want a mansion—I just want a place that smells like Mother's kitchen on Saturday.

Silly? I don't think so. After all, this place God is preparing is for *us*.

What do you remember that you want to enjoy in heaven? Think about it and then look forward to whatever wonderful thing or place or sight God may have waiting for you.

PRAYER: Dear Lord, nothing on earth will be able to compare with the magic and miracle of heaven. Help me to look forward to it.

48

WE SHALL
BE LIKE HIM

READ: 1 Corinthians 13:9-13

Then shall I know even as I am known
(1 Corinthians 13:12*b*).

Shortly after my "Heaven, I Can Hardly Wait" came out as "Heavenly Sights, Sounds and Smells" in our state-wide *Arkansas Gazette*, I received a letter I cherish.

The writer cared for her ninety-three-year-old mother. This mother, a devout Christian, had become worried and afraid of death.

The daughter related how she read my article to her mother and noticed that her mother's attitude began to change—something that no word from the daughter had been able to bring about. Instead of being fearful, the mother started to talk about the people she'd see "over there." She remembered long gone friends and was joyously looking forward to seeing them again and to meeting Bible characters she'd loved and looked up to.

Have you ever thought of heaven as a meeting place? I'll look up David. I have to know if he had red hair. I think he did. I'll shout, "Hello!" to rugged Peter; I'll blow a kiss to sweet, lovable John; and I'll tell James how much his book, which I memorized in full, has meant to me.

Would you like to know how it felt to go up to the heavens in a fiery chariot? To be "translated"? To discover the miracle of the manna? I want to seek out the little boy who watched his five loaves and two fishes divided to feed the multitude. I've written a story about him and I want to know how close I came to how he really felt that day. Was his name Zaccai? I'll call him "Zac."

Most of us would like to continue living a healthy, fruitful life—but think of the alternative. We shall know Christ. We shall be like Him. And we shall see Him face to face.

PRAYER: Oh God, how much it means to anticipate good happenings. Surely heaven is one of those. Thank You for it—in advance.

49

WHAT DOES
HEAVEN
SMELL LIKE?

READ: Philippians 4:10-20

And I saw a new heaven and a new earth
(Revelation 21:1a).

As I mentioned before, a Saturday at our house when I was a child was special to me. It always smelled so good.

I awoke to the mouth-watering scents of baking goodies—cinnamon, cloves, mint, even bread. I loved it.

When I walked to school on weekday mornings, I often caught a whiff of honeysuckle and mock orange in the spring. I also loved to sprawl on the floor of our porch enveloped in the perfume of the lilac bush just outside the screen. Fall brought a more pungent aroma matching its flamboyant colors. Everybody in our neighborhood made chili sauce. At Thanksgiving, I could hardly resist sticking my finger into one of the spicy pumpkin pies, and I found it disappointing to have to wait for the plump brown turkey to be set before Daddy and a goodly portion of it to be placed on my plate. I always put one of Mother's sweet smelling, slightly yellow, cardamom buns up to my nose before sinking my teeth into it. Fall was a specially scented season for me.

Several years later, after work, when I would open the entry hall door in our apartment building, I'm sure my nose twitched when I caught the full-flavored smell of stuffed peppers. How I hoped that aroma emanated from our flat. It usually did.

As I became a wife and explored my own ways in the kitchen, I discovered curry powder and other spices my mother never used. Even the rich, full-bodied smell of oxtail soup, fixed only because my husband told me several times how good it was, overcame my determination not to eat it (the determination arrived at as I stripped the meat from the awful looking, knotty bones).

Some people don't like their noses. I appreciate mine.

The completely individual fragrance of one beautiful rose from my husband always made me lift my face to his in visual thanks. The smell of an approaching rainstorm at sunset, an early morning walk while the air still retains a trace of its freshly bathed essence, and the sweetness of a new babe taken from its bath and covered with powder all bring a smile to my face.

Even a snowflake on my nose, sleet in my face and the winter wind off Lake Michigan offer their own special scents.

I can hardly wait for heaven. Since God is

preparing that place for me, I expect a corner that will smell like Saturday morning when I was growing up. I look forward to new, exotic, tantalizing fragrances which I've never smelled before.

If you feel a little low today, think about heaven. What aromas have you enjoyed? Where did they first make themselves known to you? What happy memories do you associate with them? What do you suppose God is getting ready for your nose?

PRAYER: Lord, I can't begin to visualize heaven. It's going to be so much more than I can imagine. Thank You, Jesus, for dying for me and promising me such a fragrant, future home with You.

50

SING A
NEW SONG

READ: Isaiah 35:4-10

Behold, my servants shall sing for joy of heart
(Isaiah 65:14*a*).

A s a musician I have some special memories.

The first time I heard Handel's *Messiah* my heart nearly burst for joy. I was so glad someone had invited our teenage group that Christmas season. As I became more familiar with the music, I was always deeply moved when our Swedish Choral Club sang, "His Yoke Is Easy, and His Burthen [Burden] Is Light." My heart still skips a beat and then hammers away as the strains of the trumpet and the soloist begin their special duet.

It pleased me when I began to study voice to hear my teacher say, "You are the only one of my sopranos who accents the word *know* in 'I Know That My Redeemer Liveth.' " I did it intentionally because it was a personal fact to me. I wanted everyone in the audience to realize I believed what I was singing.

Auditioning and being accepted into

Chicago's Swedish Choral Club was another highlight for me.

When the Swedish Choral Club was asked to join the Chicago Symphony Orchestra in Beethoven's *Ninth Symphony* with Fritz Reiner conducting, I didn't know what to expect. As we reached the end portion and began the last page, every instrument and every voice raced at full speed and loudest volume. A flick of Fritz Reiner's finger and it ceased — abruptly. Unashamed tears chased each other down my cheeks while shivers rippled up my spine. Never before, nor since, have I experienced such a choral thrill.

Another thrill awaited me at home in my own church. I'd chosen to sing "The Lord Is My Light" for the first Sunday of our new pastor's ministry with us. Always nervous until after the first phrase of a solo, I suddenly realized something different was happening this time. Not a bulletin crackled; not a whisper sounded. I couldn't even tell if the congregation breathed. God had them spellbound.

When I finished, a few moments of complete silence filled the sanctuary. Then the minister quietly rose and leaned over and whispered to me, "Thank you."

Perhaps you sing in your church. That's good. But there are also other less noticeable places where your message can be heard and blessed by God.

One night in a skid row mission I noticed a young man seated near the front. At that time, most of the men who frequented missions were much older. This young man made my heart grieve, so I prayed for him.

Just after I finished my last solo, he got up and left. I knew that if he departed before the message, he couldn't come back in. The attendant locked the outer door and refused admission to anyone.

I began wrestling with God and tears filled my eyes. As I prayed, I seemed to hear a voice say, "I can speak to him anywhere," and I relaxed. Near the end of the sermon, I noticed someone at the door and the attendant opened it. The young man entered. When the invitation was given, that young man came forward and my heart sang all the way home.

These are some of my personal moments of joy through music. All of them began when my mother cuddled me in her lap and I fell asleep to her lullaby.

Surely in heaven we will hear the vehemence of cymbals, the strident notes of a trumpet, the Heifitz-like strains of a violin, the joyousness of hallelujahs and the soft, sweet notes of a lullaby.

No tone-deaf people will walk those streets, no voices will sing flat, no monotones will be unable to sing. If God could inspire a Handel, a Beethoven, a mother, what will heaven's music be like? I don't know, but I'm anticipating something wonderful. How about you?

PRAYER: Oh Lord, granter of all talents, I expect what I hear in heaven to be far above anything I've enjoyed on earth. I believe even non-music-lovers will be won over when they arrive inside those holy gates. Thank You for all Your preparations for us. I can hardly wait.

51

FALL
IN LOVE
WITH THE MOON?!

READ: Genesis 15:1-5

One thing have I desired of the LORD . . . to behold the beauty of the LORD, and to enquire in his temple (Psalm 27:4).

One night Marilyn fell in love with the moon. That love affair has lasted almost forty years.

She and Georgia arrived in Miami Beach early that day, and after supper they sat at the poolside in the gathering dusk. Only the underwater pool lights gleamed. No one else was present.

A glow appeared on the eastern horizon, and they watched as the most enormous moon Marilyn had ever seen emerged from the sea and laid a silver carpet at their feet. Since then, Marilyn praises God every time the moon peeks through her patio door or illuminates her kitchen table.

She watched a moon sliver when Venus rode high at one corner, and she tracked the two of them as they passed in the night. The moon rose while

Venus fell.

She also holds an idea that she doesn't share with many people. "They'd think I was strange," she says. She thinks God may some day give her a star as her home.

Far-fetched? Most people would think so. However, God said the stars would be as Abraham's seed – a great many. Scientists continue to find new galaxies. Some day we may each live on a star – one of our own.

When I lived in Arkansas I loved to drive into my carport, walk around the back of my car and look up at Orion, the archer. He was almost always poised as though guarding my home. I began to look for this guardian on every fair night.

Think back on some of the beautiful sights you have seen.

Did you discover a rainbow was round after standing on the Canadian side of Niagara Falls? No wonder no one has ever found the pot of gold purported to be at its foot.

Have you seen the gorgeous beauty of fall as you travel east from Pittsburgh and approach the Alleghenies? Was it then that you realized how beautiful a tree could be?

Our God inspired Monet to show the unusual attractiveness of a common sight – haystacks.

Have you viewed some harbors? Which did you choose as the most beautiful? The one at Sydney, Australia, is my choice.

Have you caught a glimpse of Mt. Rainier from the east side? If so, you rounded a corner and there it was. Its three-peaked, snow-crowned head touches the blue of the sky. Little Lake Tipsoo nestles on its breast and tall straight evergreens, like soldiers, stand guarding her.

The Alps are indescribably beautiful. The rugged, barren terrains of Scotland speak of strength. The rushing, noisy Rhine Falls of Switzerland tumbling helter-skelter over the rocks, remind one of a mischievous child when drops of its spray land on the onlookers.

What do you remember? Equally inspiring scenes? If you do, also think about this. God is designing a heavenly home for us. He knows exactly what kind of person you are and what kind I am. He's kept a record of our likes and dislikes. Don't you believe He will top the most fantastic beauty we have seen on earth?

And, maybe, just maybe, He'll build our homes on a star.

PRAYER: Lord, make me aware of the beauty around me. Fill me with anticipation as I look forward to heaven's scenic wonders.

EPILOGUE

WHAT

SOME PEOPLE

THINK OF AGE

READ: John 8:31,32

I have been young and now am old: Yet have I not seen the righteous forsaken, nor his seed begging bread (Psalm 37:25).

Ira Wallach: "Age brings with it certain advantages. One advantage is that we have . . . more experience . . . and this helps us deal with life more easily."

Phyllis A. Whitney: "The mind . . . is the director of all that happens to us . . . To stay young . . . our minds must be constantly challenged and taught new ways."

D. Elton Trueblood: "Never ignoring or denying the physical hardship of old age, I nevertheless offer . . . the calmness and freedom of which Cephalus spoke [to Socrates in Plato's 'Republic'] are real . . . Autumn is . . . the most beautiful season of the year . . . a parable of human life, as well as a fact of nature."

Dr. Samuel Johnson: "Vernal flowers, however beautiful and gay, are only intended by nature as preparation to autumn fruits."

Sir William Mulock: "Ninety-five. It sounds old, but, strangely enough, I don't feel old at all. It's just another birthday like all the others . . . and the best of life is still ahead."

Victor Hugo: "Winter is on my head, but spring is in my heart."

What some people did when they were older:

Plato: Wrote "The Laws" at eighty.

Cato, first Latin prose writer of importance: Learned Greek at eighty.

Verdi: Produced *Falstaff* in his eightieth year.

Michelangelo: Still produced masterpieces at eighty-nine.

Goethe: Completed the second part of *Faust* at eighty-two.

Grandma Moses: Painted in her nineties.

Perhaps one of my favorite quotes for the aging is from Bernard Baruch: "To me, old age is always fifteen years older than I am."

And, sometimes I wonder, *What would Mozart have accomplished had he lived twice as long?* Well, maybe he's composing in heaven!

D. Elton Trueblood: "Real freedom comes at the end of a process rather than in the beginning."

PRAYER: Lord, help me to see the advantages as I approach my older years. Constantly challenge my mind and aid me in the enjoyment of autumn. May

I continue to learn and produce and enjoy these bonus years of freedom.

Ask your local Christian bookstore about these other new titles from Here's Life Publishers . . .

The Satanic Revival
by Mark I. Bubeck

A resurgence of devil worship has recently exploded in virtually every region of the United States. It's time for a great spiritual awakening, writes Mark Bubeck. You'll find the tools you need to equip you and your loved ones to take bold action in the war against evil. ISBN 0-89840-314-6/$8.95

Finding the Heart to Go On
by Lynn Anderson

An "inspirational masterpiece," drawing from the life of David. Bestselling author Max Lucado writes in the Foreword: "If you want to be stirred, motivated, challenged and changed, your wish is about to be granted." ISBN 0-89840-309-X/$8.95

Mara, The Woman at the Well
by Gloria Howe Bremkamp

In her first of three biblical novels for Here's Life Publishers, this noted fiction writer delivers the heart-touching story of Mara, the woman who encountered Jesus at the well. ISBN 0-89840-304-9/$7.95

"The Greatest Lesson I've Ever Learned"

By 24 noted Christian women who share their stories of the greatest lessons they have learned in life. Includes Barbara Bush, Joni Eareckson Tada, Evelyn Christenson, Ann Kiemel Anderson, Ruth Bell Graham, and many others. ISBN 0-89840-286-7/hardcover/$12.95

At Christian Bookstores Everywhere.
Or call

Here's Life Publishers
1-800-950-4457
(Visa and Mastercard accepted.)